I0212451

A HANDBOOK FOR RECITERS

# THE TRAGEDY

## A NARRATION OF THE SAGA OF KARBALA

FOREWORD BY
### SAYYID HASSAN ALHAKEEM

EDITED BY
### MOHAMED ALI ALBODAIRI

THE MAINSTAY
FOUNDATION

Foreword by: Sayyid Hassan al-Hakeem

Edited by: Mohamed Ali Albodairi

© 2018 The Mainstay Foundation

ALL RIGHTS RESERVED. No part of this work covered by the copyright may be reproduced or used in any form or by any means – graphic, electronic, or mechanical, including photocopying, recording, taping, web distribution, information storage and retrieval systems, or in any other manner – without the written permission of the Mainstay Foundation.

Printed in the United States.

ISBN: 978-1943393329

# DEDICATION

To our Beloved Twelfth Holy Imam (a)

# Contents

# Foreword

On the tenth day of the month of Muharram, fifty years after the passing of the Holy Prophet Muhammad (s), Imam Hussain (a) and a small number of family members and companions were slaughtered at the hands of the Umayyad government. They made their stance on the land of Karbala with determination and resolve. They did not waiver in the face of an army of thousands. They made that stance in the hope that their memory will bring life to a Muslim nation which was spiraling fast down the road of deviance.

More than thirteen centuries have passed since. Yet every year, Muslims around the world continue to commemorate the tragedy and remember Imam Hussain's (a) great sacrifice. Devotees from around the globe flock to his grave in Karbala to visit and supplicate. They remember the events of that bloody massacre and the valor of Imam Hussain (a) and his companions. They recite verse and prose in commemoration of that stance.

Because of the great importance of the tragedy and the passion that it infused into the Muslim nation, Umayyad authorities did all they could to erase its memory. They forbade the mentioning of Imam Hussain (a), persecuted anyone who professed love to the Holy Prophet's (s) household, and spread false ideologies that absolved them of any culpability. Despite all this, Imam Hussain's (a) stance was engraved into the conscience of the Muslim nation. As Lady Zaynab proclaimed in the court of Yazid, "By God, you will never erase our remembrance or kill our inspiration."

As a fulfilment of Lady Zaynab's promise, Muslim historians were able to compile and record the events of the tragedy with great detail. Some scholars would even dedicate entire volumes to the tragedy. These books – known as the *Maqatil* (sing. *Maqtal*) – are now the chief sources for historical accounts in regards to Imam Hussain's (a) stance on the lands of Karbala.

Each year, Muslims around the globe gather during the anniversary of Ashura to recite the saga of Imam Hussain (a) and his stance in Karbala. In many traditions, excerpts of the books of the *Maqatil* are read verbatim to a mourning crowd. Unfortunately, there has not been a comprehensive source that can be referred to for this saga in the English language. Through this work, the Mainstay Foundation hopes to provide such a resource for the English recitation of the saga.

This work is an abdridged version of *The Saga: The Battle of Karbala*, and is prepared for the specific purpose of providing reciters and lecturers with a resource to use during the mourning of Ashura. God willing, we will continue to to make annual updates and revisions to this book, allowing us to enhance what we hope to be an integral resource for the servants of Imam Hussain (a). If you have any comments or feedback you would like to share, please do not hesitate to contact us at info@mainstay.us.

In compiling this work, we were careful to ensure that all entries are properly referenced. Most entries are taken from the books of the *Maqatil* in which our scholars dedicated volumes to the memory of the battle of Karbala. Specifically, many entries are taken from:

- *Al-Saheeh min Maqtal Sayyid al-Shuhada (a)* by Muhammad al-Rayshahri,
- *Maqtal al-Hussain (a)* by Abdulrazzaq al-Muqarram,
- *Maqtal al-Hussain (a)* by al-Muwaffaq ibn Ahmad al-Khowarizmi,
- *Maqtal al-Hussain (a)* by Abu Mikhnaf,
- *Lawa'ij al-Ashjan* by Sayyid Muhsin al-Ameen, and
- *Mawsu'at Karbala* by Dr. Labeeb Beydoun.

We hope that this work is accepted by our beloved Imam Hussain (a) as a contribution to the preservation of his message and stance. We pray to God Almighty to accept our efforts and make them a means of growing closer to His service.

Finally, we want to take this opportunity to thank you for your support. As students of Islam and as compilers of this text, our greatest purpose is to please God by passing along this knowledge to others. By picking up this book, you have lent your crucial support to this endeavor. We hope that you will continue your support throughout the rest of this book, and we ask that you keep us in your prayers whenever you pick it up.

*Sayyid Hassan al-Hakeem,*

The Mainstay Foundation, London, UK

# Pre Ashura

The family members of Ahlulbayt (a)[1] started from the city of Medina then went to Mecca, and from Mecca they went to Kufa. Before they arrived to Kufa itself they were stopped by al-Hur ibn Yazid al-Reyahe. That meeting with al-Hur ibn Yazid al-Reyahe took place on the 2nd of Muharram. Al-Hur had 500 soldiers. He was sent by Ibn Zeyad.

---

[1] Alayhem al-Salaam

# Who is Yazid?

At the time Muawiyah ibn Abi Sufyan when he died he had taken control over Syria, Damascus. He was fighting Imam Ali ibn Abi Talib (a). Now, when Imam Ali (a) was martyred, Imam Hassan (a) succeeded his father. But there were many wars between Imam Hassan (a) and Muawiyah (l)[2]. And when Imam Hassan (a) was martyred, Muawiyah was trying to take over the authority of the entire Muslim world. Then and there when Muawiyah knew his time was coming close, he wanted to install Yazid, his son, as the governor and the authority over the Muslim world.

# Geography of the Muslim World

Syria is close to what is known now as Lebanon. In today's geography we have Lebanon we have Palestine we have Syria and we have Jordon. Back then in history, it was all known as balid al-sham. These four countries were given the name balid al-sham. Close to it is the country called Iraq. Iraq is still known as Iraq. To the south of it the collective countries of Saudi Arabia, Bahrain, Kuwait, Qatar, UAE, Yemen, and Oman all these together used to be known as al-hajaz and al-Yemen. These together al-hajaz and al-Yemen then there is Iraq then there is balid al-sham and to it was Persia.

Basra is in the south of Iraq. Go a little to the north that's where is the city of Kufa. Kufa was known to be a very important central city. Now to the outside, a little bit outside, of Kufa about 40 so minutes outside Kufa is where you find Karbala, the city of Karbala. That's were Imam Hussain (a) was martyred and he was left with his companions.

---

[2] la'anat Allah ta'ala 'alaih

# The Governors of Banu Umayya

Syria where Damascus is that's where Yazid ibn Muawiya was. Obaid Allah ibn Zeyad was a governor on Basra. Yazid ordered him to go from Basra to Kufa and to put the revolt down so he can make sure everything is under his leadership. Obad Allah ibn zeyad sent at the beginning the first army of 500 soldiers by Al-Hur bin Yazid a general of his army. So Al-Hur is another general of Obad Allah ibn Zeyad. Obad Allah ibn zeyad is a governor in the authority of Bany Omiya which is Yazid. Now another general that is higher in status is called Omar ibn Saad. Omar ibn saad reported to him many different generals.

# Imam Hussain's Camp

Imam Hussain (a), when he came to Karbala, some narrations say he had about 72 men. 32 of these were cavalries 40 were infantry. The Imam (a) divided his army into the following. He divided a right flank, a left flank, and the heart. Three right, left, and the heart. The right was given to the general in his army al Zuhair ibn al-Kayn. The left was given to Habib ibn Mothahar. In the heart is where Imam Hussain (a) stayed. Now back then in the wars of Arabia, there was something known as the *Raya* or the banner. The banner is very important. Usually one of the strongest warriors in the camp would carry the banner. If the banner would fall that means the army lost the war or is losing the battle. So who was given the banner? In the camp of Imam Hussain (a) it was none other than Al-Abbas ibn Ali ibn Abu Talib (a).

# Yazid's Camp

Let's look at the army of Yazid. The army of Yazid. First 4000 came with al-Hussain. Then they arrived in the 3rd day of Muharram. Then Omar ibn saad came with 4000 other. Al-Hur ibn Yazid had 1000. Now more came from another state a city called al-Qadeeseya with 3000 and it kept on adding up. In the narrations in the stories when we read in history, they say the army of yazid; some said 20,000 like historian known as ibn Tawoos, another as alalama al-Majlasi said were 30,000. Ibn Shahrashoob said 35,000 and other historians put the number up to a 100,000 soldiers in the army of Yazid. So the least is 20,000, the maximum is about to a 100,000. We have that range of in history. Why that range. Because they did not have a proper way to surveying. You'll see numbers and numbers of flanks of soldiers and they would estimate and that's what happened. Now in the army of Yazid there were the important general's Omar ibn al-Hajaj he was on the right flank, Shimr ibn thel jawshan (l) was on the left flank and on the cavalry was Ozrat ibn Qais on the infantry Shibth ibn Raba'ay and Dorad Mawla. Omar ibn Saad was given the banner.

## Arrival to Karbala

The Hur met Imam Hussain (a), al-Hur was with the camp of Yazid in the beginning. On the 2nd day of Muharram the meeting took place where they agreed not to move around just to stay around and to settle until the orders come from ibn ziyad. Now this was in the lunar year of 61 A.H. Now we are in the year 1440, so you can see there is about 1370+ years from the event of Karbala until now. On the 7th day, it is said the Omar ibn Saad ordered that the water be blocked from Ahlubayt and they should not access it. So the last time they were able to access the water it was on the 7th day.

# The Battle of Karbala

# Al-Hussain's (a) First Sermon on the Day of Ashura

ثمّ دعا براحلته فركبها ، و نادى بصوت عال يسمعه جلّهم :

Al-Hussain (a) then called for his horse. He rode his horse and called with a loud voice so that most could hear him,

أيّها النّاس اسمعوا قولي ، ولا تعجلوا حتّى أعظكم بما هو حقّ لكم عليّ ، وحتّى أعتذر إليكم من مَقدمي عليكم.

*O' people! Listen to me and do not be hasty with me until I advise you, as that is a right of yours over me, and until I give you the justification of my journey toward you.*

فإن قبلتم عذري وصدقتم قولي وأعطيتموني النّصف من أنفسكم، كنتم بذلك أسعد، ولم يكن لكم عليّ سبيل.

*If you were to accept my justification and believe my words, giving me what you know to be right, you would be the happier and you will find no reason to fight me.*

وإنْ لَم تقبلوا مِنّي العذر ولَم تعطوا النّصف من أنفسكم ، فأجمعوا أمركم وشركاءكم ثمّ لا يكن أمركم عليكم غمّة . ثمّ اقضوا إليَّ ولا تنظرون.

*But if you reject my justification and do not give me what you know to be right, then "conspire together, along with your partners, leaving nothing vague in your plan, then carry it out against me without giving me any respite" (The Holy Quran, 10:71).*

إنَّ وليّيَ اللهِ الذي نزل الكتاب وهو يتولّى الصالحين.

*"My guardian is indeed God who sent down the Book, and He takes care of the righteous" (The Holy Quran, 7:196).*

ثم حمد الله وأثنى عليه وصلّى على محمّد (ص) وعلى الملائكة والأنبياء وقال في ذلك ما لا يُحصى ذكرُه ولَم يُسمع متكلّم قبله ولا بعده أبلغ منه في منطقه ، ثمَّ قال:

He then praised God and glorified him, sent peace and blessings upon Muhammad (s), the angels, and the prophets. He said so much in this regard that it cannot all be recounted, and he spoke so eloquently that no speaker was ever heard before or after him speaking in such eloquence. He then said,

أيّها النّاس إنَّ الله تعالى خلق الدنيا فجعلها دار فناء وزوال متصرفة بأهلها حالاً بعد حال ، فالمغرور من غرّته والشقي من فتنته.

*All praise be to God who created this world and made it an abode of ruin and passing. It steers its dwellers from one state to another. The truly deceived is the one who is deceived by it. The truly wicked is the one who is mesmerized by it.*

فلا تغرّنكم هذه الدنيا ، فإنّها تقطع رجاء من ركن إليها وتُخيّب طمع من طمع فيها.

*So do not be deceived by this world. It will surely subdue the hopes of whomever indulges in it and quash the ambitions of whomever greeds for it.*

وأراكم قد اجتمعتم على أمر قد أسخطتم الله فيه عليكم وأعرض بوجهه الكريم عنكم وأحلَّ بكم نقمته.

*I can see that you agreed on a matter by which you have reaped the wrath of God, causing Him to turn His face away from you, make His curse befall you, and exile you from His mercy.*

فنِعمَ الربّ ربّنا وبئس العبيد أنتم؛ أقررتم بالطاعة وآمنتم بالرسول محمّد (ص) ، ثمّ إنّكم زحفتم إلى ذريّته وعترته تريدون قتلهم.

*The best of lords is our Lord, and the worst of servants are you! You claimed obedience [to God] and belief in His Messenger Muhammad (s). Now you march towards his offspring and progeny, intent on killing them!*

لقد استحوذ عليكم الشيطان فأنساكم ذكر الله العظيم ، فتبّاً لكم ولِما تريدون.

*Surely, Satan has taken hold over you, causing you to forget the remembrance of the Almighty God! May doom befall you and all your aspirations!*

إنّا لله وإنّا إليه راجعون هؤلاء قوم كفروا بعد إيمانهم فبُعداً للقوم الظالمين.

*From God we come and unto Him we shall all return. Surely, these are the people who have rejected faith after they had believed; so away with such an unjust lot!*

فقال ابن سعد: ويلكم كلّموه، فإنه ابن أبيه. والله لو وقف فيكم هكذا يوما جديدا لما انقطع ولما حصر. فتقدم شمر فقال: يا حسين ما هذا الّذي تقول؟ أفهمنا حتّى نفهم. فقال (ع):

Omar ibn Saad said, "Woe to you! Answer him, for by God, if he were to stand another day he would neither stop [speaking] nor would he exhaust what he has to say!" Shimr stepped forward and said, "O' Hussain (a), what is it that you are saying? Explain so that we can understand."

Al-Hussain (a) said,

لا تعجلوا، والله ما أتيتكم حتّى أتتني كتب أماثلكم، بأنّ السّنّة قد أميتت، والنفاق قد نجم، والحدود قد عطّلت، فاقدم لعل الله يصلح بك الأمة، فأتيت.

*Do not hasten against me. By God, I had not come to you except after the letters of the notables amongst you reached me saying, 'The traditions [of the Prophet (s)] had been negated, that hypocrisy has grown, and that legal punishments have been suspended, so come to us so that perhaps God may reform the nation through you.' So I came forth.*

فإذ كرهتم ذلك، فأنا أرجع.

*If that is not what you want, then I shall return from where I came.*

ثم قال (ع):

He then said,

أيها الناس، انسبوني من أنا، ثم ارجعوا إلى أنفسكم وعاتبوها، وانظروا
هل يحلّ لكم قتلي وانتهاك حرمتي؟

*O' people! Remember my bloodline and think of my pedigree.*
*Think to yourselves and admonish your conscience. Ask*
*yourselves if it is right for you to kill me.*

ألست ابن بنت نبيكم وابن وصيّه وابن عمه، وابن أول المؤمنين بالله
والمصدّق لرسول الله (ص) وبما جاء به من عند ربه؟

*Am I not the son of your Prophet's (s) daughter? Am I not*
*the son of your Prophet's (s) cousin and vicegerent? [Was my*
*father not] the first to believe in God and His Messenger who*
*delivered to you the will of his Lord?*

أو ليس حمزة سيد الشهداء عمّ أبي؟ أو ليس جعفر الطيار عمي؟

*Is Hamza, the most noble of martyrs, not my great-uncle? Is*
*Jaafar al-Tayyar the martyr not my uncle?*

أو لم يبلغكم قول رسول الله (ص) لي ولأخي: هذان سيّدا شباب
أهل الجنة؟

*Have you not heard of the words of the Messenger of God (s)*
*concerning me and my brother, "These are the two masters of*
*the youth of Paradise"?*

فإن صدّقتموني بما أقول وهو الحق، فوالله ما تعمّدت الكذب منذ
علمت أن الله يمقت عليه أهله، ويضرّ به من اختلقه.

*Believe what I say, as it is certainly true! I swear that I have not lied since I have known that God hates liars and punishes fabricators.*

و إن كذّبتموني فإن فيكم من إن سألتموه عن ذلك أخبركم.

*And if you deny what I say, ask [the educated] amongst you and they will assure you of my truthfulness.*

سلوا جابر بن عبد الله الأنصاري، وأبا سعيد الخدري، وسهيل بن سعد الساعدي، والبراء بن عازب، وزيد بن أرقم، وأنس بن مالك،

*Ask Jabir ibn Abdullah al-Ansari, Abu Saeed al-Khidari, Suhail ibn Saad al-Sa'idi, Zayd ibn Arqam, and Anas ibn Malik.*

يخبرونكم أنهم سمعوا هذه المقالة من رسول الله (ص) لي ولأخي. أما في هذا حاجز لكم عن سفك دمي؟

*They will assure you that they heard these words from the Messenger of God (s) in favor of me and my brother. Would this not give you pause and stop you from shedding my blood?*

فناداه شمر: الساعة ترد الهاوية. فقال الحسين (ع):

At this point, Shimr ibn Thiljawshan interrupted saying, "Soon you will enter hellfire!" Al-Hussain (a) said,

الله أكبر. أخبرني جدي رسول الله (ص) فقال: «رأيت كأن كلبا ولغ في دماء أهل بيتي». وما إخالك إلا إياه.

11

*God is the greatest! My grandfather, the Messenger of God (s), once told me, 'I saw [in a vision] as if a dog was licking up the blood of my family.' I do not doubt that it is you!*

فقال الشمر للحسين (ع): يا حسين بن علي، أنا أعبد الله على حرف إن كنت أدري ما تقول. فسكت الحسين (ع). فقال حبيب بن مظاهر للشمر: يا عدو الله و عدو رسوله، إني لأظنك تعبد الله على سبعين حرفا، و أنا أشهد أنك لا تدري ما يقول، فإن الله تبارك و تعالى قد طبع على قلبك. فقال له الحسين (ع):

Shimr called back, "O' Hussain ibn Ali (a), I would be worshipping God on a doubt if I knew what you are saying!" Al-Hussain (a) stayed silent, but Habib called out [to Shimr], "O' Enemy of God and enemy of His Prophet (s)! By God, I see that you worship God on seventy doubts, and I testify that you do not know what he is saying! God, the Blessed and Almighty, has surely sealed your heart [so that you do not understand]!" Al-Hussain (a) said to Habib,

حسبك يا أخا بني أسد، فقد قضي القضاء وجفّ القلم والله بالغ أمره.

*Patience, brother of Banu Asad! Judgment has been passed and the pen [of God's decree] has dried! Indeed, God will carry through His decrees!*

والله إني لأشوق إلى جدي وأبي وأمي وأخي وأسلافي، من يعقوب إلى يوسف وأخيه، ولي مصرع أنا لاقيه.

*By God, I long for my grandfather, father, mother, brother, and ancestor, a longing greater than that of Jacob for Joseph*

and his brother *[Benjamin]! Surely, I have [been decreed] a death that I will surely meet!*

ثم قال الحسين (ع):

Al-Hussain (a) then said,

فإن كنتم في شكّ من هذا القول، أفتشكّون أني ابن بنت نبيكم؟ فوالله ما بين المشرق والمغرب ابن بنت نبيّ غيري، فيكم ولا في غيركم.

*If you doubt what I have said, do you doubt that I am the son of the daughter of your Prophet (s)? By God there is no son of a prophet other than me amongst you or amongst any other nation between east and west!*

ويحكم أتطلبوني بقتيل فيكم قتلته، أو بمال استهلكته، أو بقصاص من جراحة؟

*Woe to you! Do you seek vengeance for a man I murdered? Do you seek compensation for wealth that I have damaged? Do you seek retribution for a wound I inflicted?*

فأخذوا لا يكلمونه. ثم نادى:

When no one responded he called out,

يا شبث بن ربعي ويا حجّار بن أبجر ويا قيس بن الأشعث ويا زيد بن الحارث، ألم تكتبوا إليّ أن اقدم،

*O' Shabath ibn Rab'i! O' Hajjar ibn Abjar! O' Qays ibn al-Ash'ath! O' Yazeed ibn al-Harith! Did you not all write to me [asking me to rise against Yazid]?*

فقد أينعت الثمار واخضرّ الجناب، وإنما تقدم على جند لك مجنّدة ؟!

*The fruits have ripened. The pastures have greened. The rivers*
*have swollen. [The time has come and you will find] armies*
*mustered at your command. So come forth.' [Was this not the*
*text of your letters]?*

فقالوا: لم نفعل. قال (ع):

When they denied, al-Hussain (a) exclaimed,

سبحان الله، بلى والله لقد فعلتم.

*Gracious God! Yes, by God, you did.*

ثم قال (ع):

He then said,

أيها الناس إذا كرهتموني فدعوني أنصرف عنكم إلى مأمن من الأرض.

*Oh people. If you hate me so, then let me go and I will find a*
*safe place away from you.*

فقال له قيس بن الأشعث: ما ندري ما تقول، و لكن انزل على حكم بني عمك،
فإنهم لن يروك إلا ما تحب، و لن يصل إليك منهم مكروه. فقال له الحسين
(ع):

Qays ibn al-Ash'ath asked, "Will you not come under the authority of
your kin? I swear that they will only give you what you please and they
will not harm you." al-Hussain (a) replied,

أنت أخو أخيك، أتريد أن يطلبك بنو هاشم بأكثر من دم مسلم بن عقيل؟

*You are just like your brother! Do you wish to owe the Hashemites more than the blood of Muslim ibn Aqeel?*

لا والله لا أعطيكم بيدي إعطاء الذليل ولا أقرّ فرار العبيد.

*By God! I will not give you my allegiance in disgrace. I will not submit like a slave.*

يا عباد الله إنّي عُذتُ بِرَبّي ورَبِّكُمْ أَنْ تَرْجُمُونِ [الدخان: 20]. أعوذ بربي وربكم من كل متكبر لا يؤمن بيوم الحساب.

*Oh servants of God! I seek the protection of my Lord and your Lord, if you would [dare murder] me. I seek the protection of my Lord and your Lord from the tyrant that does not believe in Judgment Day.[1]*

# Al-Hussain's (a) Second Sermon on the Day of Ashura

روي في (المناقب) بإسناده عن عبد الله بن محمّد بن سليمان بن عبد الله بن الحسن عن أبيه عن جده عن عبد الله، قال:

It is narrated in al-Manaqib by means of Abdullah ibn Muhammad ibn Sulaiman ibn Abdullah ibn al-Hassan [the following:]

لما عبّأ عمر بن سعد أصحابه لمحاربة الحسين (ع) رتّبهم مراتبهم و أقام الرايات في مواضعها، و عبّأ أصحاب الميمنة و الميسرة، و قال لأهل القلب: اثبتوا.

When Omar ibn Saad mobilized his soldiers to fight al-Hussain (a), he organized them in their flanks and raised the standards in their proper places. He mobilized the right and left flanks and told the center to stand steadfast.

و أحاطوا بالحسين (ع) من كل جانب حتّى جعلوه في مثل الحلقة. ثم ركب الحسين (ع) ناقته، و قيل فرسه، و خرج إلى الناس، فاستنصتهم فأبوا أن ينصتوا حتّى قال لهم:

They encircled al-Hussain (a) from every direction, so that [his camp] was surrounded by a ring [of enemy soldiers]. Al-Hussain (a) rode his camel - or his horse according to some narrations - and stepped forward to the people. He asked them to listen to him but they refused. He said,

ويلكم ما عليكم أن تنصتوا لي فتسمعوا قولي، وإنما أدعوكم إلى سبيل الرشاد، فمن أطاعني كان من المرشدين، ومن عصاني كان من المهلكين،

*Woe to you! What [harm] is it to you that you should listen to me and hear my words? Surely, I call you to a path of guidance. Whomever follows me is surely guided. Whomever rejects me is surely doomed.*

و كلكم عاص لأمري غير مستمع قولي، فقد ملئت بطونكم من الحرام وطبع على قلوبكم. ويلكم ألا تنصتون؟! ألا تسمعون؟!

*Yet surely, you have all rejected me and have not heard my words. Your bellies have been filled with the Haram and your hearts have been locked. Woe to you! Will you not listen? Will you not heed?*

فتلاوم أصحاب عمر بن سعد بينهم، فقالوا: أنصتوا له. فحمد الله وأثنى عليه وذكره بما هو أهله وصلى على محمّد (ص) وعلى الملائكة والأنبياء والرسل، و أبلغ في المقال، ثم قال:

Omar ibn Saad's soldiers blamed one another and said, "Let us listen to him." Al-Hussain (a) eloquently glorified God and praised him, attributing to Him what He is worthy of, and sent salutations and blessings upon Muhammad (s), the angels, the prophets, and the messengers. He then said,

تبّا لكم أيّها الجماعة وترحا!

*Woe and destruction to you all!*

أحين استصرختمونا والهين فأصرخناكم موجفين سللتم علينا سيفا لنا في أيمانكم، وحششتم علينا نارا قدحناها على عدونا وعدوكم،

*You called us in distress, but when we rushed to your aid you drew our own swords with your hands and ignited a fire against us which we had kindled against our and your common enemy.*

فأصبحتم إلبًا على أوليائكم ويدًا عليهم لأعدائكم، بغير عدل أفشوه فيكم، ولا أمل أصبح لكم فيهم،

*You have gathered against your allies and have become a tool against them in the hands of your enemies. All this was not for the sake of any justice that they instituted amongst you nor for any hopes that you may have in them.*

إلا الحرام من الدنيا أنالوكم، وخسيس عيش طمعتم فيه. من غير حدث كان منا، ولا رأي تفيّل لنا.

*Rather, it is only the Haram of this world that they have given you and a scant living which you seek. None of this was due to any offense that we have committed nor any mistaken opinion which we held.*

فهلا لكم الويلات، إذ كرهتمونا وتركتمونا، تجهّزتموها والسيف مشيم والجأش طامن والرأي لمّا يستحصف.

*Surely, woe has befallen you! If only you would have [shown your] hatred for us and deserted us while [armies were still] unreadied, swords were still sheathed, and opinions were still unsettled!*

ولكن أسرعتم إليها كطيرة الدّبا وتداعيتم إليها كتداعي الفراش،

*Yet you rushed into this like a locust swarm and were drawn into it like moths [to a flame]!*

فسحقا لكم يا عبيد الأمّة وشذّاذ الأحزاب، ونبذة الكتاب، ونفثة الشيطان، وعصبة الآثام،

*So damnation to you, O' slaveslike nation, ignoble bunch, rejectors of scripture, spew of Satan, and band of sinners!*

و محرّفي الكتاب، ومطفئي السّنن، وقتلة أولاد الأنبياء، ومبيدي عترة الأوصياء،

*[Damnation to you, O'] distorters of the Book, extinguishers of [Prophetic] tradition, killers of the sons of prophets, and murderers of the progeny of vicegerents!*

و ملحقي العهّار بالنسب، ومؤذي المؤمنين، وصراخ أئمّة المستهزئين، الذين جعلوا القرآن عضين ولبئس ما قدّمت لهم أنفسهم، وفي العذاب هم خالدون.

*[Damnation to you, O' baseborn imposters], inflictors of harm on the believers, and [responders to the] calls of the imams of derision who have made the Quran into fragments - surely evil is what they have sent ahead for their souls and Hellfire shall be their eternal abode.*

وأنتم ابن حرب وأشياعه تعضدون وعنّا تخاذلون.

*You have chosen to support the son of Harb [ibn Umayya] and desert us!*

أجل والله الخذل فيكم معروف، وشجت عليه أصولكم، وتأزّرت عليه فروعكم، وثبتت عليه قلوبكم، وغشيت صدوركم،

*Yes, by God, desertion is well-known amongst you! You have been nurtured in its ways and have worn it as a garb. Your hearts are set on it and your chests have been enveloped in darkness.*

فكنتم أخبث ثمر شجا للناظر وأكلة للغاصب. وقد جعلتم الله عليكم كفيلا، فأنتم والله هم.

*You have become the most evil fruit, inaccessible to the onlooker and an easy prey to the usurper. You have made God a guarantor [of your punishment], and by God you are surely [as I have described]!*

ألا وإن الدّعيّ ابن الدعيّ قد ركز بين اثنتين: السّلّة أو الذلّة، وهيهات منا الذلّة.

*Surely, the imposter – a son of an imposter – has [given us a choice] between death and disgrace. Surely, we will never bend to disgrace.*

يأبى الله ذلك لنا ورسوله والمؤمنون، وجدود طابت، وحجور طهرت، وأنوف حميّة، ونفوس أبيّة، لا تؤثرطاعة اللّئام على مصارع الكرام.

*God refuses that for us. So do his Messenger (s), the believers, noble ancestors, purified households, zealous souls, and proud spirits. None would prefer obedience to the wicked over a noble death.*

ألا قد أعذرت وأنذرت، ألا وإني زاحف بهذه الأسرة مع قلة العدد
وكثرة العدو، وخذلان الناصر.

*Surely, I have exceeded [my duty] and warned you [of your misdeeds]! Surely, I will march alongside with my family despite our scant numbers, the great numbers of our enemies, and the desertion of our supporters.*

ثم وصل (ع) كلامه بأبيات فروة بن مسيك المرادي، و هو صحابي مخضرم،
فقال:

He then recited the verses of Farwa ibn Musaik al-Muradi, an elder companion [of the Prophet (s)], saying,

فإن نهزم فهزّامون قدما

و إن نغلب فغير مغلبينا

*If we are defeated we were once the victors,*
*and if we are beaten, we are not always the losers.*

و ما إن طبّنا جبن ولكن

منايانا ودولة آخرينا

*We did not live in cowardice. Rather,*
*we faced our death when fortune turned to others.*

إذا ما الموت رفّع عن أناس

كلاكله أناخ بآخرينا

*If death were to turn away from some,*

*it would surely go on to others.*

فأفنى ذلكم سروات قومي

كما أفنى القرون الأولينا

*It has taken the most noble of my people,*
*just as it had taken generations past.*

فلو خلد الملوك إذا خلدنا

و لو بقي الكرام إذا بقينا

*But if kings were to live eternally, so would we.*
*And if the virtuous lived forever, we would as well.*

فقل للشامتين بنا أفيقوا

سيلقى الشامتون كما لقينا

*So let those who rejoice for our defeat wake up.*
*The gloaters will face a fate like ours.*

ثم قال:

He then continued,

أما والله لا تلبثون بعدها إلا كريث ما يركب الفرس، حتّى تدور بكم

دور الرحى وتقلق بكم قلق المحور.

*By God, you surely will not remain after this except for a*
*[short period]. Then, [the world] will turn you like the turning*
*of a millstone and will reel you the reeling of a spindle.*

22

عهد عهده إليَّ أبي عن جدي فَأَجْمِعُوا أَمْرَكُمْ وشُرَكَاءَكُمْ ثُمَّ لا يَكُنْ أَمْرُكُمْ عَلَيْكُمْ غُمَّةً ثُمَّ اقْضُوا إِلَيَّ ولا تُنْظِرُونِ [يونس: 71]

*That is a promise given to me by my father and grandfather, "So conspire together, along with your partners, leaving nothing vague in your plan, then carry it out against me without giving me any respite" (The Holy Quran, 10:71).*

ثُمَّ كِيدُونِ فَلا تُنْظِرُونِ إِنِّي تَوَكَّلْتُ عَلَى اللهِ رَبِّي ورَبِّكُمْ، ما مِنْ دَابَّةٍ إِلَّا هُوَ آخِذٌ بِناصِيتِها، إِنَّ رَبِّي عَلى صِراطٍ مُسْتَقِيمٍ [هود: 56].

*"Now try out your stratagems against me, together, without granting me any respite. Indeed I have put my trust in Allah, my Lord and your Lord. There is no living being but He holds it by its forelock. Indeed my Lord is on a straight path" (The Holy Quran, 11:55-56).*

اللَّهم احبس عنهم قطر السماء، وابعث عليهم سنين كسنيّ يوسف،

*O' God, hold back the heavens' rains and send upon them years [of drought] like the years of Joseph.*

وسلّط عليهم غلام ثقيف يسقيهم كأسا مصبّرة، ولا يدع فيهم أحدا إلا قتله، قتلة بقتلة، وضربة بضربة، ينتقم لي ولأوليائي وأهل بيتي وأشياعي منهم،

*[O' God] empower over them the man of Thaqif who will make them drink of a bitter cup so that he will spare none and kill each - one killing for another and one strike for*

*another - so that he can avenge me, my devotees, my family,
and my followers.*

فإنهم غرّونا وكذّبونا وخذلونا، وأنت ربنا عليك توكلنا وإليك أنبنا
وإليك المصير.

*Surely, they have deceived us, lied to us, and deserted us.
Surely, You are our Lord, on You we rely, to You we turn,
and to You is our final return!*

# Part of a Sermon in which Al-Hussain (a) Describes the World

ثم حمد الله و أثنى عليه و صلى على محمّد و آله، و قال:

Al-Hussain (a) praised God and glorified Him, sent salutations and prayers upon Muhammad (s) and his Progeny (a), then said,

أما بعد، فقد نزل بنا من الأمر ما قد ترون. وإن الدنيا قد تغيّرت وتنكّرت وأدبر معروفها،

*You see what has come upon us. This world has changed and become corrupted. What was commonly known as right has withered away.*

ولم يبق منها إلا صبابة كصبابة الإناء، وخسيس عيش كالمرعى الوبيل. ألا ترون إلى الحق لا يعمل به، وإلى الباطل لا يتناهى عنه،

*Nothing is left but a trace like the last few droplets of an empty cup and a lowly life like a tainted unwholesome pasture. Do you not see that truth [and righteousness] are not being acted upon [and abided by]? And that falsehood is not being discouraged?*

ليرغب المؤمن في لقاء ربه محقًّا، فإني لا أرى الموت إلا سعادة، والحياة مع الظالمين إلا برما.

*So let the believer long for meeting God. For I do not see death [for God's sake] except as happiness, and life with these oppressors except as weariness.[3]*

# Al-Hussain's (a) Sermon in which he Mentions his Lineage

ثم وثب الحسين (ع) متوكئًا على قائم سيفه، و نادى بأعلى صوته:

Al-Hussain (a) stood, leaning on his sword, and called with a loud voice,

أنشدكم الله هل تعلمون أن جدي رسول الله (ص)؟ أنشدكم الله هل تعلمون أن أمي فاطمة بنت محمّد (ص)؟

*I ask you by God, do you not know that my grandfather is Messenger of God (s)? I ask you by God, do you not know that my mother is [Lady] Fatima (a), the daughter of Muhammad (s)?*

أنشدكم الله هل تعلمون أن أبي علي بن أبي طالب (ع)؟ أنشدكم الله هل تعلمون أن جدتي خديجة بنت خويلد، أول نساء هذه الأمة إسلامًا؟

*I ask you by God, do you not know that my father is Ali ibn Abu Tali b (a)? I ask you by God, do you not know that my grandmother is Khadija bint Khuwailid, the first woman of this nation to accept Islam?*

أنشدكم الله هل تعلمون أن سيّد الشهداء حمزة عم أبي؟ أنشدكم الله هل تعلمون أن جعفرا الطيار في الجنة عمي؟

*I ask you by God, do you not know that Hamza, the Master of Martyrs, is my great-uncle? I ask you by God, do you not*

*know that Ja'far, the one granted wings in Paradise, is my uncle?*

أنشدكم الله هل تعلمون أن هذا سيف رسول الله (ص) أنا متقلده؟

أنشدكم الله هل تعلمون أن هذه عمامة رسول الله (ص) أنا لابسها؟

*I ask you by God, do you not know that this is the sword of the Messenger of God (s) that I carry? I ask you by God, do you not know that this is the turban of the Messenger of God (s) that I am wearing?*

أنشدكم الله هل تعلمون أن عليا كان أول القوم إسلاما وأعلمهم علما وأعظمهم حلما، وأنه ولي كل مؤمن ومؤمنة؟

*I ask you by God, do you not know that Ali (a) was the first individual to accept Islam, the most knowledgeable amongst the Muslims, and the greatest in wisdom amongst them? And that he is the master of every believing man and woman?*

قالوا: اللّهم نعم. قال:

To each of these questions they replied, "By God, yes!" He said,

فبم تستحلّون دمي؟ وأبي الذائد عن الحوض، يذود عنه رجالا كما يذاد البعير الصاد عن الماء، ولواء الحمد في يد أبي يوم القيامة!

*Then why are you intent on spilling my blood? Surely, my father is the protector of the Pond [of Paradise], repelling people [who are undeserving to drink of the Pond] away from it like ill camels are driven away from a watering hole. Surely, the Banner of Praise is in my father's hands on the Day of Resurrection!*

قالوا: قد علمنا ذلك كله، و نحن غير تاركيك حتّى تذوق الموت عطشا.

They replied, "We know all of this, but we shall not leave you be until you taste death while thirsty!"[4]

# Imam Hussain (a) Calling upon the People to Aid Him

ثم قال (عليه السلام):

Then [Imam Hussain (a)] said,

اشتدّ غضب الله على اليهود و النصارى إذ جعلوا له ولدا [و في رواية: اشتد غضب الله على اليهود إذ جعلوا له ولدا، و اشتدّ غضبه على النصارى إذ جعلوه ثالث ثلاثة]،

*God's anger with the Jews and the Christians was exacerbated when they ascribed a son to Him. [And in another narration, "God's anger with the Jews was exacerbated when they ascribed a son to him, and His anger with the Christians exacerbated when they made him the third in a trinity."]*

و اشتدّ غضب الله على المجوس إذ عبدت الشمس و القمر و النار من دونه، و اشتدّ غضب الله على قوم اتفقت آراؤهم [و في رواية: كلمتهم] على قتل ابن بنت نبيهم. و الله لا أجيبهم إلى شيء مما يريدونه أبدا، حتى ألقى الله و أنا مخضّب بدمي.

*And God's anger with the Zoroastrians was exacerbated when they worshiped the sun, moon, and fire in His stead. And God's anger has been exacerbated against a people whose opinion [and in another narration, "whose word"] was united in slaying the son of their prophet's daughter. By God, I will never obey them in any of their demands till I reach God [with my beard] stained by my own blood.*

ثم صاح (عليه السلام):

29

He then cried out,

ما من مغيث يغيثنا لوجه الله تعالى؟. أما من ذابّ يذبّ عن حرم
رسول الله ؟

*Is there not an aid who will aid us for the sake of God Almighty? Is there no guardian who will protect the women of [the family of] the Messenger of God (s)?*

فبكت النساء و كثر صراخهن.

At that point the women began to cry and their wails grew louder.[5]

# Imam Hussain (a) would not Begin the Battle

استعمل الحسين (عليه السلام) مختلف الوسائل الممكنة لهدي القوم و إرشادهم إلى الطريق الأقوم، و بذل جهده عسى أن يتجنّب القتال، لأنه صاحب دعوة خير و حبّ و سلام؛ دعوة الإسلام.

Imam Hussain (a) used all possible means to guide these people and lead them toward a righteous path. He exhausted his efforts in his attempts to avoid battle, as he was the carrier of a message of good, love, and peace - the message of Islam.

و كان (عليه السلام) يبغض القتل و القتال ما دام هناك طريقة بالتي هي أحسن، و لهذا كان يكره أن يبدأهم بقتال، كما قال (عليه السلام) لزهير و غيره من أصحابه في مواطن عديدة:

He hated to engage in battle and bloodshed so long as there was a way to guide by better means. That is why he would not be the one to initiate the battle. As he said to Zuhair and others of his companions on multiple occasions,

إني أكره أن أبدأهم بقتال.

*I hate to initiate battle against them.*

مقتديا بسيرة جده رسول الله (ص) و أبيه علي بن أبي طالب (عليه السلام) في دعوتهما إلى الله.

He was following the tradition of his grandfather, the Messenger of God (s), and his father, Ali ibn Abi Talib (a), in their call toward God.

و لكنه (عليه السلام) خاب ظنه فيهم، لأن الشيطان استحوذ عليهم فأنساهم ذكر الله العظيم، و ذلك عندما رشقوا معسكره بالسهام و كأنها المطر. فعندئذ لم يجد بدّا من قتالهم حتى يفيئوا إلى أمر الله. فأذن لأصحابه بالقتال، و قال لهم:

However, his hopes in these people were subverted. Satan had seized them, making them forget the remembrance of God Almighty. They launched their arrows, which rained down on the camp. At that point, he found no alternative to battle; perhaps they may then recant and come towards the path of God. He granted his companions leave to fight, saying to them,

قوموا رحمكم الله إلى الموت الّذي لا بدّ منه

*Go forth - may God have mercy on you - to your inevitable deaths.*[6]

# Imam Hussain (a) Grants His Companions Permission to Fight

فعندها ضرب الحسين (عليه السلام) بيده إلى لحيته، فقال:

Imam Hussain (a) then put his hand on his beard and said,

قوموا رحمكم الله إلى الموت الّذي لا بدّ منه، فإن هذه السهام رسل القوم إليكم.

*Go forth - may God have mercy on you - and face inevitable death, for these arrows are the people's messengers to you.*[7]

# Muslim ibn Awsaja and Nafi' ibn Hilal Enter the Battlefield

ثم خرج مسلم بن عوسجة الأسدي [...] ثم تابعه نافع بن هلال الجملي [...]

فخرج لنافع رجل من بني قطيعة، فقال لنافع: أنا على دين عثمان. فقال نافع: إذن

أنت على دين الشيطان، و حمل عليه فقتله. فأخذ نافع و مسلم يجولان في ميمنة

ابن سعد.

Then Muslim ibn Awsaja stepped forward [...] followed by Nafi' ibn Hilal al-Jamli [...]. A man from Bani Qutay'a came toward Nafi' and said, "I am on the religion of Othman." Nafi' replied, "Then you are on the religion of Satan." [Nafi'] charged towards him and killed him. Muslim and Nafi' continued to fight valiantly on the right flank of Ibn Saad's [army].[8]

# Amr ibn Al-Hajjaj Recognizes the Bravery of the Companions of Imam Hussain (a)

و أخذ أصحاب الحسين (عليه السلام) بعد أن قلّ عددهم و بان النقص فيهم،
يبرز الرجل بعد الرجل، فأكثروا القتل في أهل الكوفة. فصاح عمرو بن الحجاج
بأصحابه: أتدرون من تقاتلون؟ تقاتلون فرسان المصر و أهل البصائر و قوما
مستميتين، لا يبرز إليهم أحد منكم إلا قتلوه على قلتهم. و الله لو لم ترموهم إلا
بالحجارة لقتلتموهم.

When the ranks of Al-Hussain's (a) companions dwindled and the decrease in their numbers became evident, they began to go out one after the other [to duel]. They killed many of the Kufans. Amr ibn Al-Hajjaj called out to his companions, "Do you know who you are fighting? You are fighting 'Fursan Al-Masr' [the knights of the realms], 'Ahl Al-Basaer' [the people of insight], and a [self-sacrificing] faction. None of you will go out to duel them except that they will kill you, despite their few numbers. By God, if you were only to pelt them with stones you would kill them."

فقال عمر بن سعد: صدقت، الرأي ما رأيت. أرسل في الناس من يعزم عليهم
أن لا يبارزهم رجل منكم، و لو خرجتم إليهم وحدانا لأتوا عليكم.

Omar ibn Saad replied, "You are right; the correct opinion is yours. Send to the people someone to tell them not to go out for duels because if you go out one by one they will cut you down."[9]

# Amr ibn Al-Hajjaj Advances Against Imam Hussain's (a) Right Flank

و حمل عمرو بن الحجاج على ميمنة أصحاب الحسين (عليه السلام) فيمن كان
معه من أهل الكوفة. فلما دنا من أصحاب الحسين (عليه السلام) جثوا له على
الرّكب، و أشرعوا بالرماح نحوهم، فلم تقدم خيلهم على الرماح، فذهبت الخيل
لترجع، فرشقهم أصحاب الحسين (عليه السلام) بالنبل، فصرعوا منهم رجالا و
جرحوا منهم آخرين.

Amr ibn Al-Hajjaj advanced along with his battalion of Kufans against
the right flank of Al-Hussain's (a) camp. When he came near to Al-
Hussain's (a) companions, they dropped to their knees and lifted their
pikes. The horses did not charge the raised pikes and turned to retreat
instead. Al-Hussain's (a) companions then pelted them with arrows,
killing some and wounding others.

و كان عمرو بن الحجاج يقول لأصحابه: قاتلوا من مرق من الدين، و فارق
الجماعة. فصاح الحسين (عليه السلام):

Amr ibn Al-Hajjaj would call on to his companions, "Fight those who
have deviated from the religion and diverted away from unity." Al-
Hussain (a) called in reply,

ويحك يا حجّاج أعليّ تحرّض الناس؟ أنحن مرقنا من الدين و أنت تقيم
عليه؟!. ستعلمون إذا فارقت أرواحنا أجسادنا من أولى بصليّ النار!

*Woe to you, O' Hajjaj! Do you rouse the people against me? Is it we
who have deviated from the religion while you are its guardian? Surely,
when our souls leave our bodies you will know who is truly deserving of
dwelling in hellfire![10]*

# The Martyrdom of Muslim ibn Awsaja

ثم حمل عمرو بن الحجاج من نحو الفرات فاقتتلوا ساعة، و فيها قاتل مسلم ابن عوسجة، فشدّ عليه مسلم بن عبد الله الضبابي و عبد الله بن خشكارة البجلي و ثارت لشدة الجلاد غبرة شديدة، و ما انجلت الغبرة إلا و مسلم صريعا و به رمق. فمشى إليه الحسين (عليه السلام) و معه حبيب بن مظاهر الأسدي، فقال له الحسين (عليه السلام):

Then Amr ibn Al-Hajjaj advanced from the direction of the Euphrates, where the parties clashed for some time. Muslim ibn Awsaja was amongst the warriors and he was faced by Muslim ibn Abdullah Al-Dababi and Abdullah ibn Khashkara Al-Balji. The battle grew so fierce that a thick cloud of dust was stirred. The dust did not settle until Muslim [ibn Awsaja] was felled, laying with some life in him. Al-Hussain (a) walked to him along with Habib ibn Mudhahir Al-Asadi. Al-Hussain (a) said to [Muslim],

رحمك الله يا مسلم فَمِنْهُمْ مَنْ قَضَى نَحْبَهُ وَ مِنْهُمْ مَنْ يَنْتَظِرُ وَ ما بَدَّلُوا تَبْدِيلًا

*May God have mercy on you. 'There are some among them who have fulfilled their pledge, and some of them who still wait, and they have not changed in the least.' [The Holy Quran, 33:23]*

و دنا منه حبيب و قال: عزّ عليّ مصرعك يا مسلم، أبشر بالجنة. فقال قولا ضعيفا: بشّرك الله بخير. قال حبيب: لو لم أعلم أني في الأثر لأحببت أن توصي إليّ بكل ما أهمّك. فقال له مسلم: بل أوصيك بهذا [و أشار إلى الحسين (عليه

السلام)] أن تموت دونه. فقال: أفعل و ربّ الكعبة فما أسرع من أن مات رضوان الله عليه.

Habib drew close to [Muslim] and said, "Your death has take a toll on me, O' Muslim. I give you glad tidings of paradise." [Muslim] replied faintly, "May God give you glad tidings of all that is good." Habib then said, "If I did not know that I am following in your footsteps I would have liked for you to instruct me in regards to everything that is of consequence [as a last will and testament]." Muslim replied, "My will is this man [and he pointed to Imam Hussain (a)] and that you die aiding him." [Habib] said, "By the Lord of the Ka'ba, I will." [Muslim] quickly perished, may God be content with him.[11]

# Shimr Advances Against Imam Hussain's (a) Left Flank

ثم تراجع القوم إلى الحسين (عليه السلام)، فحمل شمر بن ذي الجوشن في الميسرة، على أهل الميسرة، فثبتوا له و طاعنوه. و حمل على الحسين (عليه السلام) و أصحابه من كل جانب. و قاتلهم أصحاب الحسين (عليه السلام) قتالا شديدا، فأخذت خيلهم تحمل، و إنما هي اثنان و ثلاثون فارسا، فلا تحمل على جانب من خيل الكوفة إلا كشفته.

Then Al-Hussain's (a) companions withdrew close to him. Shimr ibn Thiljawshan advanced against the left flank. They stood firmly and fought him. [The Umayyad army] advanced against Al-Hussain (a) from every direction. The companions of Al-Hussain (a) fought valiantly, advancing with their cavalry which consisted of thirty two horses. They advanced against the cavalry of Kufa and repelled [the Kufans] every time.[12]

# The Martyrdom of Abdullah ibn Omair al-Kalbi and his Wife Umm Wahab

و حمل الشمر في جماعة من أصحابه على ميسرة الحسين فثبتوا لهم حتى كشفوهم، و فيها قاتل عبد الله بن عمير الكلبي [و هو عبد الله بن عمير بن عباس بن عبد قيس بن عليم بن جناب الكلبي العليمي أبو وهب] فقتل تسعة عشر فارسا و اثني عشر راجلا، و شدّ عليه هانئ بن ثبيت الحضرمي فقطع يده اليمنى، و قطع بكر بن حي ساقه، فأخذ أسيرا و قتل صبرا. و ذكر الطبري في تاريخه أنه كان القتيل الثاني من أصحاب الحسين (عليه السلام).

Al-Shimr and a number of his companions charged against al-Hussain's (a) left flank, but they remained perseverant until they repelled the advance. Abdullah ibn Omair al-Kalbi fought in that confrontation, killing nineteen cavalrymen and twelve infantrymen. Hani ibn Thubayt al-Hadrami charged at him and severed his right hand. Bakr ibn Hai severed his leg. He was taken captive and killed. Al-Tabari mentioned in his account that [Abdullah] was the second of al-Hussain's (a) companions to fall.

فمشت إليه زوجته أم وهب (بنت عبد الله من النمر بن قاسط) و جلست عند رأسه تمسح الدم عنه و تقول: هنيئا لك الجنة، أسأل الله الّذي رزقك الجنة أن يصحبني معك. فقال الشمر لغلامه رستم: اضرب رأسها بالعمود، فشدخه و ماتت و هي أول امرأة قتلت من أصحاب الحسين (عليه السلام).

His wife, Umm Wahab (bint Abdullah, from the family of al-Nimr ibn Qasit), came to him. She sat by his head, wiped his blood, and said, "May you enjoy paradise! I ask God who has granted you paradise to allow me to be with you." Al-Shimr said to his servant Rustum, "Strike her head with a pole." He bashed her head and killed her, making her the first female killed from the companions of al-Hussain (a).

و قطع رأس عبد الله و رمي به إلى جمة الحسين (عليه السلام)، فأخذته أمه و مسحت الدم عنه، ثم أخذت عمود خيمة و برزت إلى الأعداء، فردّها الحسين (عليه السلام) و قال:

Abdullah's head was severed and thrown toward al-Hussain (a). His mother took his head and wiped the blood off it. She took a pole from a tent and charged toward the enemy. Al-Hussain (a) stopped her, saying,

ارجعي رحمك الله، فقد وضع عنك الجهاد.

*Return [back to the tent], may God have mercy on you, for fighting is not obligatory for you.*

فرجعت و هي تقول: اللهم لا تقطع رجائي. فقال الحسين (عليه السلام):

She returned, saying, "O' God, do not crush my hopes!" Al-Hussain (a) said to her,

لا يقطع الله رجاءك.

*God will not crush your hopes.[13]*

# Shabath ibn Rib'i Confesses to his Men's Wretchedness

و لما رأى عزرة بن قيس و هو على الخيل الوهن في أصحابه و الفشل كلما يحملون، بعث إلى عمر بن سعد يستمده الرجال. فقال ابن سعد لشبث بن ربعي: ألا تقدم إليهم؟ قال: سبحان الله، تكلف شيخ المصر، و عندك من يجزي عنه؟

When Uzra ibn Qays who commanded [an Umayyad] cavalry [regiment] saw the weakness of his men and the failure of every charge, he sent a missive to Omar ibn Saad asking for backup. Ibn Saad said to Shabath ibn Rib'i, "Would you go to aid them?" [Shabath] replied, "Glory to God! You would command the master of these lands when there are others who would suffice?"

و لم يزل شبث بن ربعي كارها لقتال الحسين، و قد سمع يقول في إمارة مصعب: قاتلنا مع علي بن أبي طالب و مع ابنه من بعده [يعني الحسن] آل أبي سفيان خمس سنين، ثم عدونا على ولده و هو خير أهل الأرض، نقاتله مع آل معاوية و ابن سمية الزانية؟! ضلال يا لك من ضلال. و الله لا يعطي الله أهل هذا المصر خيرا أبدا، و لا يسددهم لرشد.

Shabath detested fighting al-Hussain (a) and was heard saying, "We fought alongside Ali ibn Abi Talib (a) and his son [al-Hassan (a)] after him against the family of Abu Sufyan for five years. Now we have turned against his son [al-Hussain (a)] who is the best of the people of the earth, siding against him with the family of Muawiya and the son of Sumayya the adultress? Perversion! Oh the perversion! By God, God will not give the people of this land any good nor support them with any foresight."

فمدّه بالحصين بن نمير في خمسمائة من الرماة.

[Omar ibn Saad] sent al-Hossayn ibn Numair to support [Uzra ibn Qays], along with five hundred archers.[14]

# The Martyrdom of Abu al-Sha'tha' al-Kindi

و كان أبو الشعثاء الكندي- و هو يزيد بن زياد بن مهاصر الكندي- مع ابن
سعد، فلما ردّوا الشروط على الحسين (عليه السلام) صار معه. فقاتل بين
يديه، و جعل يرتجز [....] و كان راميا، فجثا على ركبتيه بين يدي الحسين (عليه
السلام) و رمى بمئة سهم ما أخطأ منها بخمسة أسهم، و الحسين (عليه السلام)
يقول:

Abu al-Sha'tha' al-Kindi (his name being Yazid ibn Ziyad ibn Muhasir al-Kindi) was in the ranks of Ibn Saad's army. When [the Umayyad army] rejected al-Hussain's (a) conditions, he joined his camp. He fought in al-Hussain's (a) ranks and [charged with chants of pride in his ancestry and dedication to al-Hussain (a)]. He was an archer, so he sat on his knees in al-Hussain's (a) camp and shot one hundred arrows - less than five of which missed their marks. All the while al-Hussain (a) would say,

اللهم سدّد رميته، و اجعل ثوابه الجنة.

*O' God, guide his shots and reward him with paradise.*

فلما نفدت سهامه قام و هو يقول: لقد تبيّن لي أني قتلت منهم خمسة. ثم حمل
على القوم فقتل تسعة نفر حتى قتل (رحمه الله).

When he ran out of arrows he stood up and said, "It seems that I have killed five of them." He then charged against the enemy and killed nine soldiers before being killed - may God have mercy on his soul.[15]

# The Martyrdom of Burair ibn Khudair

ثم برز برير بن خضير الهمداني و هو [يرتجز] و كان برير من عباد الله الصالحين،

و كان زاهدا عابدا، و كان أقرأ أهل زمانه، و كان يقال له سيّد القرّاء، و كان

شيخا تابعيا، و له في الهمدانيين شرف و قدر.

Burair ibn Khudair al-Hamadani then stepped forward unto the
battlefield [reciting verses in praise of his ancestry]. Burair was a
righteous servant of God; an austere worshipper who was foremost
amongst reciters [of the Holy Quran] during his time. He used to be
called 'the Master of Reciters.' He was an elder and a Tabi'i [i.e. he was
not himself a companion of the Holy Prophet (s), but was a student of
Imam Ali (a) and the righteous companions], with great status and
honor amongst the Hamadanis.

نادى يزيد بن معقل: يا برير كيف ترى صنع الله بك؟ فقال: صنع الله بي خيرا

و صنع بك شرا. فقال يزيد: كذبت و قبل اليوم ما كنت كذّابا، أتذكر يوم كنت

أماشيك في (بني لوذان) و أنت تقول: كان معاوية ضالا و إن إمام الهدى علي

بن أبي طالب؟ قال برير: بلى أشهد أن هذا رأيي.

"Yazid ibn Ma'qil called out, 'O' Burair! How have you found what
God has done to you?' [Burair] replied, 'God has done good by me and
left you to your evil.' Yazid said, 'You lie, and you have never been a
liar before! Do you remember when I was walking beside you in [the
lands of] Bani Lawthan and you said, "Muawiya is misguided and the
Imam of guidance is Ali ibn Abi Talib"?' Burair replied, 'Yes, I do attest
that as my view!'

فقال يزيد: و أنا أشهد أنك من الضالين. فدعاه برير إلى المباهلة، فرفعا أيديهما

إلى الله سبحانه يدعوانه أن يلعن الكاذب و يقتله. ثم تضاربا فضربه برير على

رأسه ضربة قدّت المغفر و الدماغ، فخرّ كأنما هوى من شاهق، و سيف برير
ثابت في رأسه.

Yazid said, 'I do attest that you are misguided!' Burair then called him
to a *mubahala*,[*] each raising his hand and praying that God Almighty
would curse the liar and lead him to his death. They charged at one
another and fought until Burair struck [Yazid on the head] splitting his
helmet and skull. He fell as if he was thrown off a cliff while Burair's
sword was stuck in his skull.

و بينا هو يريد أن يخرجه إذ حمل عليه (رضي بن منقذ العبدي) و اعتنق بريرا
و اعتركا، فصرعه برير و جلس على صدره، فاستغاث رضي العبدي بأصحابه،
فذهب كعب بن جابر الأزدي ليحمل على برير، فصاح به زهير بن أبي الأخنس:
هذا برير بن خضير القارئ الّذي كان يقرئنا القرآن في جامع الكوفة،

And while Burair was attempting to extract his sword, Radi ibn
Munqith al-Abdi attacked him, tackling him to the ground and
wrestling him. Burair beat him and sat on his chest, so Radi al-Abdi
called on his companions for help. Ka'b ibn Jabir al-Azdi charged at
Burair while Zuhair ibn Abi al-Akhnas called out, 'That is Burair ibn
Khudair, the reciter who used to recite the Quran to us in the Mosque
of Kufa!'

---

[*] A *mubahala* is a type of debate where two sides of an issue pray to God for the
damnation of the lying side. God says in the Holy Quran, "Should anyone argue with
you concerning him, after the knowledge that has come to you, say, 'Come! Let us
call our sons and your sons, our women and your women, our souls and your souls,
then let us pray earnestly, and call down Allah's curse upon the liars.'" (The Holy
Quran, 3:61)

فلم يلتفت إليه و طعن بريرا في ظهره، فبرك برير على رضي العبدي [...] و ألقاه كعب برمحه عنه و ضربه بسيفه فقتله (رضوان الله عليه). [...] و ذكر الخوارزمي أن الّذي قتله هو بحير بن أوس الضبّي.

But [Ka'b] did not heed his cry and stabbed Burair in the back. Burair fell on Radi al-Abdi [...]. Ka'b then used his spear to move Burair off and struck him with a sword, killing him. [...]"

Al-Khawarizmi recounts that his killer was actually Buhair ibn Aws al-Dabbi.[16]

# Al-Hurr enters the Battlefield

ثم قال الحر للحسين (عليه السلام): يابن رسول الله، كنت أول خارج عليك
فاذن لي أن أكون أول قتيل بين يديك فلعلي أن أكون ممن يصافح جدك محمدا
(ص) غدا في القيامة. فقال له الحسين (عليه السلام):

Al-Hurr then said to al-Hussain (a), "O' son of the Messenger of God,
I was the first to set out against you, so give me permission to be the
first one to die in your support. Perhaps that would [grant me the
honor to] shake the hands of your grandfather Muhammad (s) on the
Day of Resurrection." Al-Hussain (a) replied,

**إن شئت فأنت ممن تاب الله عليه، و هو التواب الرحيم.**

*As you wish. You are of those whom God has [accepted their] repentence,
and He is the Ever Relenting, the All Merciful.*

فكان أول من تقدم إلى براز القوم و هو يرتجز [...]و خرج الحر بن يزيد الرياحي
و معه زهير بن القين يحمي ظهره، فكان إذا شدّ أحدهما و استلحم شدّ الآخر
و استنقذه، ففعلا ذلك ساعة.

He was the first to duel the enemy [reciting in verse his resolve to
protect al-Hussain (a)]. Al-Hurr set out with Zuhair ibn al-Qayn
guarding his back. If either of them found himself in trouble, the other
would charge to the rescue. They continued to fight for an hour or
so.[17]

# Al-Hurr Battles Yazid ibn Sufyan

قال: فبينا الناس يتجاولون و يقتتلون، و الحر بن يزيد يحمل على القوم مقدما،

و يتمثل بقول عنترة [...] و إن فرسه لمضروب على أذنيه و حاجبه، و إن دماءه

لتسيل. فقال الحصين ابن تميم- و كان على شرطة عبيد الله- ليزيد بن سفيان:

هذا الحر بن يزيد الّذي كنت تتمنى [قتله، فهل لك به]!

Men were engaged in heated battle as al-Hurr ibn Yazid charged valiantly toward the enemy reciting the verses of Antarah [ibn Shaddad, a pre-Islamic Arab warrior-poet]. His horse was wounded at the ear and brows, with blood flowing [over its face]. Al-Hossayn ibn Tameem, who was Ubaydillah's police captain, said to Yazid ibn Sufyan, "This is al-Hurr ibn Yazid who you were hoping [to kill. Can you take him on]!"

قال: نعم. فخرج إليه، فقال له: هل لك يا حر بن يزيد في المبارزة؟ قال: نعم قد

شئت، فبرز له. قال: فأنا سمعت الحصين بن تميم يقول: و الله لبرز له فكأنما

كانت نفسه في يده، فما لبّثه الحر حين خرج إليه أن قتله [و قتل أربعين فارسا

و راجلا].

He said yes, set out towards [al-Hurr], and sid to him, "Do you, O' Hurr ibn Yazid, wish to duel?" He replied, "Yes, I do," and proceeded toward him. [The narrator, Abu Zuhair al-Absi,] said, "Then I heard Al-Hossayn ibn Tameem say, 'By God, [al-Hurr dueled] as if his soul is in his grasp [i.e. he fought with great valor, undawnted by certain death].' It was not long before [al-Hurr] finished off [his foe]."[18]

# The Martyrdom of al-Hurr ibn Yazid al-Riyahi

ثم رمى أيوب بن مشرح الخيواني فرس الحر بسهم فعقره و شبّ به الفرس،
فوثب عنه كأنه ليث و بيده السيف. فقاتلهم راجلا قتالا شديدا و هو [يرتجز]
و جعل يضربهم بسيفه حتى قتل نيفا و أربعين رجلا.

Ayoub ibn Mashrah al-Khaywani then shot al-Hurr's horse [on the knee], hamstringing it. The horse fell, but he jumped off it like a lion with the sword in his hand. He fought valiantly on foot [while reciting verses of poetry taunting and intimidating his foes]. He fought them with his sword until he killed forty-some men.

ثم حملت الرجالة على الحر و تكاثروا عليه، فاشترك في قتله أيوب بن مشرح،
فاحتمله أصحاب الحسين (عليه السلام) حتى وضعوه أمام الفسطاط الّذي
يقاتلون دونه ... و هكذا كان يؤتى بكل قتيل إلى هذا الفسطاط، و الحسين
(عليه السلام) يقول:

The [Umayyad] infantry gathered against al-Hurr and overpowered him. [A group of enemy soldiers, including] Ayoub ibn Mashrah, collaberated in killing him. Al-Hussain's (a) companions carried him and placed him in front of the tent [at the forefront of the camp]. Whenever any of the martyrs was brought to the tent al-Hussain (a) would say,

**قتلة مثل قتلة النبيين و آل النبيين.**

*A death like the deaths of the prophets and the families of the prophets.*

ثم التفت الحسين (عليه السلام) إلى الحر و كان به رمق، فقال له و هو يمسح
الدم عنه:

Al-Hussain (a) turned to al-Hurr while he still held his last breath. He wiped the blood off him and said,

أنت الحر كما سمّتك أمك، و أنت الحرّ في الدنيا و الآخرة.

*You are al-Hurr [i.e. the free] like your mother named you! You are free in this world and the next!*

و رثاه رجل من أصحاب الحسين (عليه السلام)، و قيل علي بن الحسين (عليه السلام)، و قيل إنها من إنشاء الإمام الحسين (عليه السلام) خاصة فقال:

One of the companions of al-Hussain (a) - with some historians saying that it was Ali ibn al-Hussain (a) or al-Hussain (a) himself - mourned him with the following verses,

لنعم الحرّ حرّ بني رياح * * * صبور عند مشتبك الرماح

و نعم الحر إذ نادى حسين * * * فجاد بنفسه عند الصباح

*Glory to al-Hurr, the free-man of Bani Riyah*
*He was patient amidst the clashing of spears*
*Glory to al-Hurr, who heard the cry of Hussain (a)*
*And sacrificed himself that early morn!*

# Al-Shimr stabs the Tent and Tries to Burn the Camp

و حمل القوم بعضهم على بعض، و اشتد بينهم القتال. فصبر لهم الحسين (عليه السلام) و أصحابه، حتى انتصف النهار، و هم يقاتلون من جهة واحدة. فلما رأى ابن سعد ذلك أمر بإحراق الخيم.

The two sides charged at one another and the battle raged on between them. Al-Hussain (a) and his companions persevered until mid-day, while they were battling their foe from one direction. When Ibn Saad saw this, he gave orders to burn the tents [as they had stopped his troops from flanking al-Hussain (a) and his companions].

فقال الحسين (عليه السلام) لأصحابه: دعوهم فإنهم لن يصلوا إليكم.

*Al-Hussain (a) said to his companions, "Let them be, for they will not reach you."*

ثم حمل الشمر حتى طعن فسطاط الحسين، و نادى: علي بالنار لأحرق بيوت الظالمين (فصحن النساء و خرجن من الفسطاط). فحمل عليه أصحاب الحسين حتى كشفوه عن الخيمة. فناداه الحسين (عليه السلام):

Al-Shimr charged until he stabbed al-Hussain's (a) tent, calling, "Give me a fire so I can burn the tents of the oppressors." The women cried and ran out of the tent, until the companions of al-Hussain (a) charged at [al-Shimr] and repelled him from the camp. Al-Hussain then called out [to al-Shimr],

ويلك يا شمر تريد أن تحرق خيمة رسول الله ؟!

*Woe to you, Shimr. Do you wish to burn the tent of the Messenger of God?*

قال: نعم. فرفع الحسين طرفه إلى السماء، و قال:

[Al-Shimr] replied, "Yes!" Al-Hussain (a) raised his eyes to the heavens and said,

اللهم لا يعجزك شمر أن تحرقه بالنار يوم القيامة.

*O' God, Shimr will not stop you from burning him on the Day of Resurrection!*[19]

# Hamid ibn Muslim Denounces Shimr's Action

و روي عن حميد بن مسلم (قال) قلت لشمر بن ذي الجوشن: سبحان اللّه،
إن هذا لا يصلح لك؛ أتريد أن تجمع على نفسك خصلتين: تعذّب بعذاب اللّه،
و تقتل الولدان و النساء؟! و اللّه إن في قتلك الرجال لما ترضي به أميرك.
(قال) فقال: من أنت ؟ (قال) قلت: لا أخبرك من أنا. قال: و خشيت و اللّه
أن لو عرفني أن يضرني عند السلطان!

It is narrated that Hamid ibn Muslim said, "I said to Shimr ibn Thiljawshan, 'Glory to God! That is unbecoming of you. Do you wish to garner two traits; that you incur God's torment, and that you kill women and children? By God, surely killing the men will be enough please your master [Yazid].' He said to me, 'And who are you?' I replied, 'I will not tell you who I am.' By God, I feared that if he knew me, he would speak ill of me to those with authority."[20]

# Shabath ibn Rib'i Disparages Shimr

قال: فجاءه رجل كان أطوع له مني (شبث بن ربعي) فقال له: ما رأيت مقالا

أسوأ من قولك، و لا موقفا أقبح من موقفك! أمرعبا للنساء صرت! قال: فأشهد

أنه استحيا فذهب لينصرف.

[Hamid ibn Muslim] said, "Then a man who he listened to more than
me - Shabath ibn Rib'i - came and said, 'I have not heard a statement
worse than yours, nor a stance worse than yours! Have you become a
terrorizer of women!' I swear that he was ashamed and left at once."[21]

# Zuhair ibn al-Qayn Rescues the Tents

و حمل عليه زهير بن القين في رجال من أصحابه عشرة، فشدّ على شمر بن ذي الجوشن و أصحابه؛ فكشفهم عن البيوت، حتى ارتفعوا عنها.

Zuhair ibn al-Qayn took ten of his companions and charged against Shimr ibn Thiljawshan and his men. They repelled them from the camp and saved the tents.[22]

# The Martyrdom of Amr ibn Khalid al-Azdi and His Son

و برز عمرو بن خالد الأزدي و هو [يرتجز] ثم قاتل حتى قتل رحمة الله عليه.
فتقدم ابنه خالد بن عمرو، و هو يرتجز [...]فلم يزل يقاتل حتى قتل رحمة الله
عليه.

Amr ibn Khalid al-Azdi charged into the battlefield [reciting verses of poetry in supplication to God Almighty]. He fought until he was killed - may God bless his soul. Then his son Khalid ibn Amr stepped forward, [reciting verses in glorification of God Almighty]. He fought until he was killed - may God bless his soul.[23]

# The Martyrdom of a Group of Companions

و أما عمرو بن خالد الصيداوي و سعد مولاه، و جابر بن الحارث السلماني و مجمع بن عبد الله العائذي، فإنهم قاتلوا في أول القتال، فشدّوا مقدمين بأسيافهم على أهل الكوفة، فلما أوغلوا فيهم عطف عليهم الناس و قطعوهم عن أصحابهم.

As for Amr ibn Khalid al-Saydawi and his servant Saad, Jabir ibn al-Harith al-Salmani, and Majma' ibn Abdullah al-'A'ethi, they had fought at the beginning of the battle, charging with their swords against the people of Kufa. When they charged deep inside enemy lines, the soldiers circled around them and cut them off from their companions.

فندب إليهم الحسين (عليه السلام) أخاه العباس (عليه السلام) فاستنقذهم بسيفه و قد جرحوا بأجمعهم. و في أثناء الطريق اقترب منهم العدو فشدوا بأسيافهم مع ما بهم من الجراح، و قاتلوا حتى قتلوا أول الأمر في مكان واحد.

Al-Hussain (a) sent al-Abbas to aid them, but they had already been wounded. While on the way back, they saw the enemy approaching and so they charged despite their wounds. They fought until they were killed together in the same spot.

و عاد العباس (عليه السلام) إلى أخيه و أخبرهم بخبرهم. و كان هؤلاء الأربعة من مخلصي الشيعة في الكوفة، التحقوا بالحسين (عليه السلام) بالعذيب قبل وصوله إلى كربلاء.

Al-Abbas returned to his brother and told him what had happened. These four were of the devout Shia of Kufa, having joined the caravan of al-Hussain (a) at the 'Atheeb al-Hijanat [on the outskirts of modern day Najaf] before he reached Karbala.[24]

# The Battle Continues Until Mid-day

و كان القتل يبين في أصحاب الحسين (عليه السلام) لقلة عددهم، و لا يبين في أصحاب عمر بن سعد لكثرتهم. و اشتدّ القتال و التحم، و كثر القتل و الجراح في أصحاب أبي عبد الله الحسين (عليه السلام) إلى أن زالت الشمس.

Each casualty seemed to show on al-Hussain's (a) camp; his companions were so few in the first place. On the other hand, the casualties of the day did not seem to show on the amry of Omar ibn Saad due to its massive numbers. The battle raged on and the number of martyrs and wounded continued to increase until the sun reached its zenith.[25]

# Abu Thumama Remembers the Prayer

و رأى أبو ثمامة الصائدي زوال الشمس، فقال للحسين (عليه السلام): يا أبا

عبد الله نفسي لك الفدا، أرى هؤلاء قد اقتربوا، و لا و الله لا تقتل حتى أقتل

دونك، و أحب أن ألقى ربي و قد صليت هذه الصلاة التي دنا وقتها. فرفع

الحسين (عليه السلام) رأسه إلى السماء و قال له:

Abu Thumama saw that the sun was approaching its zenith. He said to
al-Hussain (a), "May my life be sacrificed for yuo, O' Abu Abdullah (a)!
I see [the enemy] coming closer, and by God you will not be killed
before I die protecting you. But I would love to meet my Lord after
perfomring this prayer whose time is approaching." Al-Hussain (a)
raised his eyes to the sky and said,

ذكرت الصلاة جعلك الله من المصلين، نعم هذا أول وقتها، سلوهم أن

يكفّوا عنا حتى نصلي.

*You have remembered prayer, may God make you amongst the
worshipers [on the Day of Judgment]! Yes, this is the beginning of its
time. Ask them to halt their advance so that we may pray.*

فقال له الحصين بن نمير: إنها لا تقبل منك! فقال له حبيب بن مظاهر: لا تقبل

الصلاة زعمت من آل رسول الله و تقبل منك يا ختّار؟!

[The companions did so, but] al-Hossayn ibn Numair replied, "It will
not be accepted from you!" Habib ibn Mudhahir retorted, "You claim
that it will not be accepted from the family of the Messenger of God
(s) and that it will be accepted from a miscreant like you?!"

[...] فلما فرغ [أبو ثمامة] من الأذان نادى الحسين (عليه السلام):

[...] When [Abu Thumama] finished the Athan, al-Hussain (a) called out,

يا عمر بن سعد أنسيت شرائع الإسلام، ألا تكفّ عنا الحرب حتى نصلي؟!

*O' Omar ibn Saad, have you forgoten the teachings of Islam! Would you stop your advance so that we may pray?*

فلم يجبه عمر. فناداه الحصين بن نمير: يا حسين صلّ فإن صلاتك لا تقبل! فقال له حبيب بن مظاهر: ويلك لا تقبل صلاة الحسين و تقبل صلاتك يابن الخمّارة؟! فحمل عليه الحصين، فضرب حبيب وجه فرسه بالسيف فشبّت به و وقع عنها الحصين، فاحتوشه أصحابه فاستنقذوه.

Omar did not reply, but al-Hossayn ibn Numair said, "O'Hussain (a), pray for your prayer will not be accepted!"

"Woe to you! Al-Hussain's (a) prayer is not accepted, while yours is, O' son of a drunkard?!" replied Habib ibn Mudhahir. Al-Hossayn charged at him, but Habib struck his horse on its face with his sword. The horse threw al-Hossayn and he fell to the ground, but he was rescued by his men.[26]

# The Martyrdom of Habib ibn Mudhahir

ثم خرج حبيب بن مظاهر و عمره ينوف على الخامسة و السبعين، و قاتل

قتالا شديدا، فقتل على كبره اثنين و ستين رجلا، و هو [يرتجز] و حمل عليه

بديل بن صريم فضربه بسيفه، و طعنه آخر من تميم برمحه، فسقط إلى الأرض.

Habib ibn Mudhahir then set out to the battlefield. He was an elder
man, seventy five years of age. Yet he fought valiantly and killed 62
men despite his age, [reciting verses lauding the virtues of his
companions as he swept the battlefield]. Badeel ibn Suraym charged at
him and struck him with his sword. Another man from Tameem
stabbed him with his spear, forcing him to the ground.

فذهب ليقوم و إذا الحصين بن نمير يضربه بالسيف على رأسه، فسقط لوجهه،

و نزل إليه التميمي و احتزّ رأسه. فهدّ مقتله الحسين (عليه السلام) فقال:

He attempted to get up, but al-Hossayn ibn Numair struck him on his
head with a sword. He fell to the ground again, [with al-Hossayn
having dealt him his final blow]. The man from Tameem rushed to
him and severed his head. Habib's martyrdom overwhelmed al-Husain
(a), who would say,

عند الله أحتسب نفسي و حماة أصحابي.

*It is in God that I place my hopes [of retribution for my murder and the
murder of] my valiant companions.*

و استرجع كثيرا. و في (مقتل الحسين المنسوب لأبي مخنف) ص 66: ثم قال

الحسين (عليه السلام):

He continued to repeat [the Holy Verse, "Indeed we belong to God and to Him do we indeed return."] And in Abu Mikhnaf's *Maqtal* (p. 66), "Al-Hussain (a) then said,

لله درّك يا حبيب، لقد كنت فاضلا تختم القرآن في ليلة واحدة.

*May God accept your work, O' Habib! You were a man of virtue, reciting the entire Quran in a single night."*

و قيل: قتله بديل بن صريم.

It is also said that he was killed by Badeel ibn Suraym.[27]

# Zuhair ibn al-Qayn Enters the Battlefield

لما قتل [...] حبيب بن مظاهر بان الانكسار في وجه الحسين (عليه السلام)

[...] فقام إليه زهير بن القين و قال: بأبي أنت و أمي يابن رسول الله ما هذا

الانكسار الّذي أراه في وجهك، ألست تعلم أنا على الحق ؟ قال:

When [...] Habib had been martyred, al-Hussain (a) was overwhelmed with grief [...]. Zuhair ibn al-Qayn stood close to al-Hussain (a) and said, "May my mother and father be sacrificed for you, O' son of the Messenger of God! What is the disheartenment I see in your face? Do you not know that we are in the right?" Al-Hussain (a) replied,

بلى و إله الخلق، إني لأعلم علماً يقيناً أني و إياكم على الحق و الهدى.

*Yes, I swear by the Lord of Creation! I know with absolute certainty that you and I are on a path of truth and guidance!*

فقال زهير: إذا لا نبالي و نحن نصير إلى الجنة و نعيمها. ثم تقدم أمام الحسين

فقال: يا مولاي أتأذن لي بالبراز ؟ فقال:

Zuhair said, "Then we will not worry, as we will soon enter paradise and enjoy its splendors!" He then stood in front of al-Hussain (a) and said, "My lord, do you grant me leave to join the battle?" Al-Hussain (a) said,

ابرز.

*[Yes,] go out into the battlefield.*

قال: ثم حمل على القوم، و لم يزل يقاتل حتى قتل خمسين فارسا، و خشي أن

تفوته الصلاة مع الحسين (عليه السلام) فرجع و قال: يا مولاي إني خشيت

أن تفوتني الصلاة فصلّ بنا.

He charged against the enemy and fought until he killed twenty knights. But he feared that he would miss the prayer alongside al-Hussain (a), so he returned and said, "My lord, I feared that I might miss prayer, so lead us [in this last prayer before our death]."[28]

# Noon Prayer

فقال الحسين (عليه السلام) لزهير بن القين و سعيد بن عبد الله الحنفي:

Al-Hussain (a) said to Zuhair ibn al-Qayn and Saeed ibn Abdullah al-Hanafi,

تقدّما أمامي حتى أصلي الظهر.

*Stand in front of me so that I can pray the noon prayers.*

فتقدما أمامه في نحو من نصف أصحابه، حتى صلّى بهم صلاة الخوف. و يقال: إنه صلى و أصحابه فرادى بالإيماء.

They stood in front of him along with about half of his companions so that he can pray *Salat al-Khawf.*[*] It is also said that al-Hussain (a) and his companions prayed individually through gestures, [a form of *Salat al-Khawf* performed in times of extreme fear].[29]

---

[*] *Salat al-Khawf* is a special method of performing the obligatory daily prayers while in times of fear, especially during war.

# Post noon

# The Martyrdom of Saeed ibn Abdullah al-Hanafi

فوصل إلى الحسين (عليه السلام) سهم، فتقدم سعيد بن عبد الله و وقف يقيه من النبال بنفسه، و ما زال يرمى بالنبل و لا تخطئ، فما أخذ النبل الحسين (عليه السلام) يمينا و شمالا إلا قام بين يديه، فما زال يرمى حتى سقط إلى الأرض، و هو يقول: اللهم العنهم لعن عاد و ثمود و أبلغ نبيك عني السلام، و أبلغه ما لقيت من ألم الجراح، فإني أردت بذلك ثوابك في نصرة ذرية نبيك. و التفت إلى الحسين (عليه السلام) قائلا: أوقّيت يابن رسول الله ؟

[While al-Hussain (a) was leading prayer], an arrow struck him. Saeed ibn Abdullah al-Hanafi stepped forward and began to shield al-Hussain (a) with his own body from a barrage of arrows. Whenever an arrow came toward al-Hussain (a) from left or right, Saeed lept to shield him. He continued to take arrows until he fell to the ground saying, "O' God, curse them like you cursed the people of 'Ad and Thamud. Send peace and blessings upon Your Prophet (s), and inform him of the wounds that I have taken. Surely, I only wanted Your reward by supporting the progeny of Your Prophet (s)." He turned to al-Hussain (a) and said, "Have I fulfilled my duty, O' son of the Messenger of God (s)?" Al-Hussain (a) replied,

## قال: نعم أنت أمامي في الجنة.

*Al-Hussain (a) replied, "Yes, and you shall walk in front of me into paradise."*

(و في رواية) أنه قال: اللهم لا يعجزك شيء تريده، فأبلغ محمدا (ص) نصرتي و دفعي عن الحسين (عليه السلام)، و ارزقني مرافقته في دار الخلود. ثم قضى

نحبه (رضوان الله عليه)، فوجد في جسمه ثلاثة عشر سهماً، سوى ما به من ضرب السيوف و طعن الرماح.

Another narration stated that Saeed said, "O' God, You are never deterred against anything that You want! Inform Muhammad (s) of my support and protection of al-Hussain (a) and grant me his company in the Eternal Abode." After he passed away - may God bless his soul - thirteen arrows were found on his body in addition to the cuts of the swords and the stabs of the spears [that he suffered during battle].[30]

# Al-Hussain (a) Gives Glad Tidings to His Companions

فلما فرغ (عليه السلام) من صلاة الظهر قال لأصحابه:

After the prayer al-Hussain (a) said to his companions,

يا كرام هذه الجنة قد فتّحت أبوابها و اتصلت أنهارها و أينعت ثمارها و زيّنت قصورها و تؤلّفت ولدانها و حورها. و هذا رسول الله (ص) و الشهداء الذين قتلوا معه، و أبي و أمي، يتوقعون قدومكم عليهم، و يتباشرون بكم و هم مشتاقون إليكم.

*O' most noble [companions]! This is paradise; its gates are open, its rivers are flowing, its fruits are ripe, its palaces are decorated, and its servants and maidens are delighted [for your arrival]! This is the Messenger of God (s) and the martyrs killed beside him, along with my father and mother, awaiting for your arrival! They joyously pass word of your coming and long for your arrival.*

فحاموا عن دينكم و ذبّوا عن حرم رسول الله (ص) و عن إمامكم و ابن بنت نبيكم، فقد امتحنكم الله تعالى بنا، فأنتم في جوار جدنا و الكرام علينا و أهل مودتنا، فدافعوا بارك الله فيكم عنا.

*So defend your faith and protect the family of the Messenger of God (s) and your Imam and the son of your Prophet's (s) daughter! God Almighty has tested you with us! You are in proximity of our grandfather [the Prophet (s)], honored by us, and the people of affection toward us! So defend us, may God bless you!*

فلما سمعوا ضجوا بالبكاء و النحيب و قالوا: نفوسنا دون أنفسكم و دماؤنا دون

دمائكم و أرواحنا لكم الفداء. و الله لا يصل إليكم أحد بمكروه و فينا الحياة و

قد وهبنا للسيوف نفوسنا، و للطير أبداننا، فلعلنا نقيكم زحف الصفوف، و

نشرب دونكم الحتوف، فقد فاز من كسب اليوم خيرا، و كان لكم من المنون

مجيرا.

When they heard this, they began to wail and cry. They said, "Let our
lives be taken rather than yours! Let our blood be spilled rather than
yours! May our souls be sacrificed for you! By God, no one will reach
you with any harm while we still live! We have pledged ourselves to the
sword and our bodies to [scavenging] birds, so that perhaps we may
protect you from the march of this army and taste death instead of
you! Victorious is he who acts righteously today and protects you
against impending death!"[31]

# Omar ibn Saad Hamstrings al-Hussain's (a) Horses

ثم إن عمر بن سعد وجّه عمرو بن سعيد في جماعة من الرماة فرموا أصحاب الحسين (عليه السلام) حتى عقروا خيولهم و لم يبق مع الحسين فارس إلا الضحاك بن عبد الله المشرقي. يقول: لما رأيت خيل أصحابنا تعقر أقبلت بفرسي و أدخلتها فسطاطا لأصحابنا.

Omar ibn Saad directed Amr ibn Saeed along with a group of archers to pelt al-Hussain (a) and his companions until their horses were killed or hamstrung. No knight remained on his steed except for al-Dahhak ibn Abdullah al-Mashriqi who said, "When I saw my companions horses being hamstrung, I took my horse and stowed it in a tent."

و اقتتلوا أشد القتال. و كان كل من أراد الخروج، ودّع الحسين (عليه السلام) بقوله: السلام عليك يابن رسول الله، فيجيبه الحسين (عليه السلام):

[Al-Hussain's (a) companions] continued to fight valiantly. Whenever one of them wanted to set out into battle, he would bid farewell to al-Hussain (a) by saying, "Peace be upon you O' son of the Messenger of God (s)." Al-Hussain (a) would reply,

و عليك السلام و نحن خلفك، فَمِنْهُمْ مَنْ قَضَى نَحْبَهُ وَ مِنْهُمْ مَنْ يَنْتَظِرُ وَ ما بَدَّلُوا تَبْدِيلًا [الأحزاب: 23].

*Peace be upon you, and we will follow you. 'There are some among them who have fulfilled their pledge, and some of them who still wait, and they have not changed in the least' (The Holy Quran, 33:23)[32]*

# The Martyrdom of Abu Thumama

و خرج أبو ثمامة الصائدي فقاتل حتى أثخن بالجراح. و كان مع عمر بن سعد
ابن عم له يقال له قيس بن عبد الله بينهما عداوة، فشدّ عليه و قتله، رضوان الله
عليه.

Abu Thumama al-Sa'edi stepped forth onto the battle field and faught
until he was weakened by his wounds. He had a cousin named Qays
ibn Abdullah in the army of Omar ibn Saad and there was some enmity
between them. [Qays] charged at [Abu Thumama] and killed him - may
God bless his soul.[33]

# The Martyrdom of Zuhair ibn al-Qayn

ثم خرج زهير بن القين البجلي و هو [يرتجز] و روي أن زهيرا لما أراد الحملة، وقف على الحسين (عليه السلام) و ضرب على كتفه و قال:

Zuhair ibn al-Qayn then set out into the battlefield, reciting [verses announcing his dedication to al-Hussain (a) and the family of the Prophet (s)]. It is narrated that when Zuhair wanted to join the battle, he stood before al-Hussain (a), put his hand on his shoulder, and recited,

اقدم حسين هاديا مهديّا * * * اليوم تلقى جدّك النبيا

و حسنا و المرتضى عليّا * * * و ذا الجناحين الفتى الكميّا

و أسد الله الشهيد الحيّا

*Go forth, Hussain (a), O' guided guide*

*Today you will meet your grandfather the Prophet (s)*

*And Hassan (a) and the Chosen Ali (a)*

*And the winged man, [Jafar al-Tayyar]*

*And the Lion of God, the living martyr [Hamza]*

[...] فقال الحسين (عليه السلام):

[...] Al-Hussain (a) said,

**و أنا ألقاهما على أثرك.**

*[Go forth] and I shall meet them soon after you.*

ثم قاتل قتالا شديدا، فشدّ عليه كثير بن عبد الله الشعبي و مهاجر بن أوس التميمي، فقتلاه. فقال الحسين (عليه السلام) حين صرع زهير:

He fought valiantly until Katheer ibn Abdullah al-Shi'bi and Muhajir ibn Aous al-Tameemi charged at him and killed him. When Zuhair was martyred al-Hussain (a) said,

لا يبعدنّك الله يا زهير، و لعن الله قاتلك، لعن الذين مسخهم قردة و خنازير.

*May God never distance you [from His mercy], O' Zuhair. May God curse those who have killed you like he cursed those who he deformed into apes and pigs.*[34]

# The Martyrdom of Amr ibn Qaradha al-Ansari

و خرج عمرو بن قرظة الأنصاري، فاستأذن الحسين (عليه السلام) فأذن له.
فبرز و هو يرتجز [...]فقاتل قتال المشتاقين إلى الجزاء، و بالغ في خدمة سلطان
السماء، حتى قتل جمعا كثيرا من حزب ابن زياد، و جمع بين سداد و جهاد.

Amr ibn Qaradha al-Ansari stepped forward and asked al-Hussain (a)
for permission to fight. Al-Hussain (a) granted him permission, so he
joined battle reciting [verses the declared his intent to defend al-
Hussain (a)]. He fought like those longing for their reward and excelled
in the service of the Lord of the Heavens. He killed many of the army
of Ibn Ziyad, combining both righteous deeds and excellent combat.

و جاء عمرو بن قرظة الأنصاري و وقف أمام الحسين (عليه السلام) يقيه العدو
و يتلقى السهام بصدره و جبهته، فلم يصل إلى الحسين (عليه السلام) سوء. و
لما كثر فيه الجراح التفت إلى أبي عبد الله (عليه السلام) و قال: أوفيت يابن
رسول الله ؟ قال:

Amr ibn Qaradha then stood in front of al-Hussain (a) in order to
protect him from the enemy and their barrage of arrows. He took the
arrows with his chest and head so that no harm could reach al-Hussain
(a). When his wounds grew too many, he turned to al-Hussain (a) and
said, "Have I fulfilled my duty, O' son of the Messenger of God (s)?"
Al-Hussain (a) replied,

نعم أنت أمامي في الجنة، فأقرئ رسول الله مني السلام و أعلمه أني
في الأثر.

*Yes, and you are entering paradise before me. Give my peace and greetings to the Messenger of God (s) and tell him that I will soon follow you.*

و خرّ ميّتا (رضوان الله عليه). فنادى أخوه علي بن قرظة و كان مع عمر بن سعد: يا حسين يا كذاب، غررت أخي حتى قتلته ؟! فقال (عليه السلام):

Amr fell to the ground and passed away, may God bless his soul. His brother, Ali ibn Qaradha, who was in the army of Omar ibn Saad called out, "Hussain (a) you liar! You deceived my brother until you killed him!" Al-Hussain (a) replied,

إني لم أغرّ أخاك، و لكن الله هداه و أضلّك.

*I did not deceive your brother, but God guided him and left you in your misguidance.*

فقال: قتلني الله إن لم أقتلك. ثم حمل على الحسين (عليه السلام) ليطعنه فاعترضه نافع بن هلال الجملي، فطعنه حتى صرعه.

"May God kill me if I dont kill you," Ali ibn Qaradha said as he charged at al-Hussain (a). Nafi' ibn Hilal al-Jamali intercepted him and killed him [before he could reach al-Hussain (a)].[35]

# The Martyrdom of Nafi' ibn Hilal

ثم خرج نافع بن هلال الجملي و جعل يرميهم بالسهام فلا تخطئ، و كان خاضبا

يده، و كان يرمي [ويرتجز] فلم يزل يرميهم حتى فنيت سهامه. ثم ضرب إلى

قائم سيفه فاستلّه، و حمل و هو يقول:

Nafi' ibn Hilal al-Jumali then stepped forward and began to pelt the
enemies with [poisoned] arrows and would not miss. He would
continue to shoot and recite [verses taunting his enemies] until his
arrows were depleted. He then drew his sword and charged at the
enemy, reciting,

أنا الغلام اليمنيّ الجملي * * * ديني على دين حسين و علي

إن أقتل اليوم فهذا أملي * * * و ذاك رأيي و ألاقي عملي

*I am a Yemeni, Jumali man*

*My creed is that of Hussain (a) and Ali (a)*

*If I were killed today, that would be my wish*

*This is my belief, and I will soon see the results of my deeds*

[...]فأحاطوا به يرمونه بالحجارة و النصال حتى كسروا عضديه و أخذوه أسيرا،

فأمسكه الشمر و معه أصحابه يسوقونه. فقال له ابن سعد: ما حملك على ما

صنعت بنفسك؟. قال: إن الله يعلم ما أردت. فقال له رجل و قد نظر إلى

الدماء تسيل على وجهه و لحيته: أما ترى ما بك؟!

[...] The enemies surrounded him, pelting him with rocks and arrows
until they broke his arms and took him prisoner. Al-Shimr and his
companions took him and dragged him [to Omar ibn Saad who] asked,
"What drove you to do this to yourself?" He replied, "God knows what

I wanted." A man that saw his blood pouring over his face and beard said to him, "Do you not see what has happened to you?"

فقال: و الله لقد قتلت منكم اثني عشر رجلا سوى من جرحت، و ما ألوم

نفسي على الجهد، و لو بقيت لي عضد ما أسرتموني. و جرّد الشمر سيفه، فقال

له نافع: و الله يا شمر لو كنت من المسلمين لعظم عليك أن تلقى الله بدمائنا،

فالحمد لله الّذي جعل منايانا على يدي شرار خلقه. ثم قدّمه الشمر و ضرب

عنقه.

He said, "By God, I have killed twelve of you and wounded others. I do not regret my efforts, and if I had an arm left [unbroken] you would not have captured me." Al-Shimr drew his sword, so Nafi' said to him, "By God, O' Shimr, if you were a Muslim you would have feared to meet God with our blood on your hands. Praise God who made our deaths at the hands of the most evil of his creation." Al-Shimr pushed him forward and struck him on his neck, [killing him].[36]

# The Martyrdom of John the Servant of Abu Thar al-Ghafari

ثم خرج جون مولى أبي ذر الغفاري، و هو شيخ كبير السن من الموالي ، فجعل يحمل عليهم [وهو يرتجز] ووقف جون مولى أبي ذرّ الغفاري أمام الحسين (عليه السلام) يستأذنه، فقال (عليه السلام):

Then John, the servant of Abu Thar al-Ghafari and an elderly black man, charged at the enemy [taunting his enemies and praising al-Hussain (a) in verse]. John stood in front of al-Hussain (a) and asked permission to fight. Al-Hussain (a) said,

**إنما تبعتنا طلبا للعافية، فأنت في إذن مني.**

*O' John, you followed us in hopes of a good outcome, so you have my permission [to leave the camp if you wish].*

فوقع على قدميه يقبّلهما و يقول: أنا في الرخاء ألحس قصاعكم، و في الشدة أخذلكم!. و الله إن ريحي لنتن، و حسبي للئيم، و لوني لأسود، فتنفّس عليّ بالجنة، ليطيب ريحي، و يشرف حسبي، و يبيضّ وجهي. لا و الله لا أفارقكم حتى يختلط هذا الدم الأسود مع دمائكم. فأذن له الحسين. فقتل 25 شخصا حتى قتل (رضوان الله عليه).

John fell on al-Hussain's (a) feet and said, "In times of ease I eat from your food, but in times of hardship I would desert you! By God, my odor is rancid, my lineage is base, and my complexion is black. Breathe over me in paradise so that my odor would become pleasant, my lineage would become noble, and my face would become bright. No, by God I will not leave you until this blood mixes with your blood."

Al-Hussain (a) gave him permission to join battle. He killed twenty five enemy soldiers before being killed - may God bless his soul.

(و في رواية أبي مخنف في مقتله، ص 71) قال: «فلم يزل يقاتل حتى قتل سبعين رجلا، فوقعت في محاجر عينه ضربة، و كبا به جواده إلى الأرض، فوقع على أمّ رأسه، فأحاطوا به من كل جانب و مكان، فقتلوه». فوقف (عليه السلام) و قال:

Abu Mikhnaf narrates in his *Maqtal* (p. 71) :He continued to fight until he killed seventy men. Then a strike hit him on the eye and he fell off his horse to the ground, falling on his head. Enemy soldiers surrounded him and killed him. [Al-Hussain (a)] stood over his body and said,

اللهم بيّض وجهه و طيّب ريحه و احشره مع محمّد (ص) و عرّف بينه و بين آل محمّد (ص).

*O' God, brighten his face, refine his odor, and grant him an abode with Muhammad (s) in the hereafter and alongside the family of Muhammad (s).*

و روي عن الإمام الباقر (عليه السلام): أن الناس كانوا يحضرون المعركة فيدفنون القتلى، فوجدوا جونا بعد عشرة أيام تفوح منه رائحة المسك.

It is narrated that Imam al-Baqir (a) said, "Peolple used to come to the battlefield and bury their dead. They found John's body ten days after the battle with his body emitting an aroma of musk."[37]

# The Remaining Companions Race for Martyrdom

فلما رأى أصحاب الحسين (عليه السلام) [أنهم قد غلبوا] و أن الأعداء قد كثروا، و أنهم لا يقدرون على أن يمنعوا حسينا (عليه السلام) و لا أنفسهم، تنافسوا في أن يقتلوا بين يديه.

When al-Hussain's (a) companions saw that they had been beaten, that the enemies remain numerous, and that they will not be able to defend al-Hussain (a) or even themselves, they began to race toward martyrdom before him.[38]

# The Martyrdom of Handhala ibn As'ad al-Shabami

ثم جاء إليه حنظلة بن أسعد العجلي الشبامي فوقف بين يدي الحسين (عليه السلام) يقيه السهام و الرماح و السيوف بوجهه و نحره، و أخذ ينادي:

Then Handhala ibn As'ad al-Shabami stepped forward and stood in front of al-Hussain (a), shielding him against arrows, swords, and spears with his own body. He cried out [the verses of the Holy Quran],

يا قَوْمِ إِنِّي أَخَافُ عَلَيْكُمْ مِثْلَ يَوْمِ الأَحْزَابِ. مِثْلَ دَأْبِ قَوْمِ نُوحٍ وَ عَادٍ وَ ثَمُودَ وَ الَّذِينَ مِنْ بَعْدِهِمْ وَ مَا اللَّهُ يُرِيدُ ظُلْماً لِلْعِبَادِ. وَ يا قَوْمِ إِنِّي أَخَافُ عَلَيْكُمْ يَوْمَ التَّنَادِ. يَوْمَ تُوَلُّونَ مُدْبِرِينَ ما لَكُمْ مِنَ اللَّهِ مِنْ عَاصِمٍ وَ مَنْ يُضْلِلِ اللَّهُ فَما لَهُ مِنْ هادٍ.

*'O' my people! Indeed I fear for you [a day] like the day of the [heathen] factions; like the case of the people of Noah, of 'Ad and Thamud, and those who came after them, and God does not desire any wrong for [His] servants. O' my people! I fear for you a day of mutual distress calls, a day when you will turn back [to flee], not having anyone to protect you from God, and whomever God leads astray has no guide' (The Holy Quran, 40:30-33).*

و يا قوم لا تقتلوا حسينا فيسحتكم الله بعذاب وَ قَدْ خابَ مَنِ افْتَرَى. فقال له الحسين (عليه السلام):

"O' my people, do not kill Hussain (a) and elicit the punishment of God, 'Whoever fabricates lies certainly fails' (The Holy Quran, 20:61)." Al-Hussain (a) said to him,

يا ابن أسعد رحمك الله، إنهم قد استوجبوا العذاب حين ردّوا عليك ما دعوتهم إليه من الحق، و نهضوا إليك يشتمونك و أصحابك، فكيف بهم الآن و قد قتلوا إخوانك الصالحين!

*O' Ibn As'ad, may God have mercy on you! They had become deservant of punishment when they answered your call toward truth [earlier] by cursing you and your companions. What do you expect of them now after they have killed your righteous brethren!*

فقال: صدقت جعلت فداك، أفلا نروح إلى ربنا فنلحق بإخواننا! فقال له الحسين (عليه السلام):

Handhala replied, "True, may I be sacrificed for you! Then shall we not head towards our Lord and join our brethren?" Al-Hussain (a) said,

**رح إلى ما هو خير لك من الدنيا و ما فيها، و إلى ملك لا يبلى.**

*Go forth to what is better for you then the entirety of the world and what is in it. [Go forth] to a kingdom that will never perish.*

فقال: السلام عليك يا ابن رسول الله، و على أهل بيتك، و جمع الله بيننا و بينك في الجنة. فقال الحسين (عليه السلام):

Handhala said, "Peace be upon you, O' son of the Messenger of God (s), and upon your family. May God unite us again in paradise." Al-Hussain (a) replied,

**آمين آمين.**

*Amen, amen.*

ثم تقدم فقاتل قتالا شديدا، فحملوا عليه فقتلوه.

Handhala stepped forward and fought valiantly, but the enemies charged at him and killed him.[39]

# The Martyrdom of Shawthab the Servant of Bani Shakir

و أقبل عابس بن شبيب الشاكري و معه شوذب مولى بني شاكر. و كان شوذب من الرجال المخلصين، و داره مألف للشيعة يتحدثون فيها فضل أهل البيت (عليهم السلام). فقال: يا شوذب ما في نفسك أن تصنع؟. قال: أقاتل معك دون ابن بنت رسول الله (ص) حتى أقتل.

Abis ibn Shabeeb al-Shakiri approached alongside Shawthab, the servant of Bani Shakir. Shawthab was a loyal man and his house was a hub for the Shia in which they recited the virtues of the Holy Household (a). Abis said, "O' Shawthab, what would you like to do?" Shawthab replied, "I will fight by your side in defense of the son of the Messenger of God's (a) daughter until I am killed."

قال: ذلك الظن بك، فتقدم بين يدي أبي عبد الله (عليه السلام) حتى يحتسبك كما احتسب غيرك، و حتى أحتسبك أنا، فإن هذا يوم نطلب فيه الأجر بكل ما نقدر عليه، فإنه لا عمل بعد اليوم، و إنما هو الحساب. فتقدم شوذب فقال: السلام عليك يا أبا عبد الله و رحمة الله و بركاته، أستودعك الله. ثم قاتل حتى قتل.

Abis said, "Just as expected from you! Go forth before Abu Abdullah (a) so that he may grieve for you just as he grieved for the others, and so that I may grieve for you as well. This is a day in which we do all we can to attain the rewards [of God Almighty], for there are no deeds after today - only judgment awaits." Shawthab stepped forward and said, "May the peace, mercy, and blessings of God be upon you, O' Abu Abdullah (a). I leave you in God's care!" He fought until he was killed.[40]

# The Martyrdom of Abis ibn Shabeeb al-Shakiri

و جاء عابس بن شبيب الشاكري، فتقدم و سلّم على الحسين (عليه السلام) و قال له: يا أبا عبد الله، أما و الله ما أمسى على ظهر الأرض قريب و لا بعيد أعزّ عليّ و لا أحبّ منك. و لو قدرت على أن أدفع عنك الضيم و القتل بشيء أعزّ عليّ من نفسي و دمي لفعلت! السلام عليك يا أبا عبد الله، أشهد أني على هداك و هدى أبيك. ثم مشى بالسيف نحوهم.

Abis ibn Shabeeb al-Shakiri stepped forward and greeted al-Hussain (a). He said, "O' Abu Abdullah (a), by God night has not fell on anyone atop this earth - near of kin or not - more dear and beloved to me than you! If I were able to repel evil and death from you with anything more valuable than my life and blood, I surely would! Peace be upon you, O' Abu Abdullah. I witness that I am a follower of your guidance and the guidance of your father." He approached the enemy with his sword.

قال ربيع بن تميم: فلما رأيته مقبلا عرفته- و قد كنت شاهدته في المغازي فكان أشجع الناس- فقلت للقوم: أيها الناس، هذا أسد الأسود، هذا ابن شبيب، لا يخرجنّ إليه أحد منكم. فأخذ ينادي: ألا رجل؟ ألا رجل لرجل! فتحاماه الناس لشجاعته. فقال لهم عمر بن سعد: ارضخوه بالحجارة فرموه بالحجارة من كل جانب. فلما رأى ذلك ألقى درعه و مغفره، و شدّ على الناس فهزمهم بين يديه.

Rabi' ibn Tameem said, "When I saw him coming, I recognized him; having seen him in battle fighting as the bravest of men. I said to the people, 'This is the valiant lion! This is Ibn Shabeeb! Let none of you fight him [alone].'" Abis cried out, "Are there no men amongst you who would fight man to man?" The enemies evaded him because of what they knew of his bravery. Omar ibn Saad said to them,

"Overpower him with stones!" They pelted him with stones from every direction. Abis threw his shield and helmet and charged at them, repelling them away.

(قال الراوي): فو الله لقد رأيته يطرد أكثر من مئتين من الناس، ثم أحاطوا به من كل جانب فقتلوه، فرأيت رأسه في أيدي الرجال، كلّ يقول: أنا قتلته.

The narrator said, "By God, I saw him repelling more than two hundred men until they surrounded him from every direction and killed him. I saw his head passed about by soldiers, each crying, 'I killed him!'"[41]

# The Martyrdom of Saad ibn Handhala al-Tameemi

ثم خرج من بعده سعد بن حنظلة التميمي، و هو [يرتجز] ثم حمل و قاتل قتالا
شديدا، حتى قتل (رضوان الله عليه).

After [the martyrdom of Abis], Saad ibn Handhala al-Tameemi joined the battle, reciting [verses of encouragement to inspire himself and his companions]. He charged and fought valiantly until he was killed - may God bless his soul.[42]

# The Martyrdom of Omair ibn Abdullah al-Mithhiji

ثم خرج من بعده عمير بن عبد الله المذحجي، و هو [يرتجز] و لم يزل يقاتل

قتالا شديدا، حتى قتله مسلم الضبابي و عبد الله البجلي، اشتركا في قتله.

Then Omair ibn Abdullah al-Mithhiji stepped forward into the battlefield, [chanting verses that declare his bravery and taunt his enemies]. He continued to fight valiantly until he was killed by Muslim al-Dababi and Abdullah al-Bajali.[43]

# The Martyrdom of Abdulrahman al-Yazani

ثم خرج عبد الرحمن بن عبد الله اليزني، و هو [يرتجز] ثم حمل فقاتل حتى
قتل (رضوان الله عليه).

Then Abdulrahman ibn Abdullah al-Yazani stepped forward, [reciting verses of his commitment to his cause]. He charged at the enemy and fought until he was killed - may God bless his soul.[44]

# The Martyrdom of Yahya ibn Saleem al-Mazini

ثم خرج من بعده يحيى بن سليم المازني، و هو [يرتجز] ثم حمل فقاتل حتى قتل
(رضوان الله عليه).

Then Yahya ibn Saleem al-Mazini stepped forward, reciting [verses of poetry to taunt his enemies]. He charged at the enemy and fought until he was killed - may God bless his soul.[45]

# The Martyrdom of Qurra ibn Abu Qurra al-Ghafari

ثم خرج من بعده قرّة بن أبي قرة الغفاري، و هو [يرتجز] ثم حمل فقاتل حتى قتل (رضوان الله عليه).

Then Qurra ibn Abu Qurra al-Ghafari joined the battle, [announcing in verse his unwavering commitment to protect the family of the Prophet (s)]. He charged at the enemy and fought until he was killed - may God bless his soul.[46]

# The Martyrdom of Anas ibn al-Harith al-Kahili

و كان أنس بن الحارث بن نبيه الكاهلي شيخا كبيرا صحابيا، رأى النبي (ص) و

سمع حديثه، و شهد معه بدرا و حنينا. فاستأذن الحسين (عليه السلام) و برز

شادّا وسطه بالعمامة، رافعا حاجبيه بالعصابة. و لما نظر إليه الحسين (عليه

السلام) بهذه الهيئة بكى، و قال:

Anas ibn al-Harith ibn Nabeeh al-Kahili was an elder companion who had seen the Prophet (s) and carried his traditions, witnessing the battles of Badr and Hunayn alongside the Prophet (s). He took permission from al-Hussain (a) and joined the battle with his turban wrapped around his abdomen [to support his back] and his eyebrows tied back with a band. When al-Hussain (a) saw him like this, he wept and said,

شكر الله سعيك يا شيخ.

*May God reward your efforts, O' shaykh.*

ثم حمل و لم يزل يقاتل حتى قتل على كبره ثمانية عشر رجلا، و قُتِلَ أَمَامَ

الحسين (عليه السلام).

He charged at the enemy and fought until he killed eighteen men despite his old age, before being slain before al-Hussain's (a) eyes.[47]

# The Martyrdom of Amr ibn Muta' al-Ju'fi

ثم خرج من بعده عمرو بن مطاع الجعفي، و هو [يرتجز] و لم يزل يقاتل حتى قتل ثلاثين رجلا، ثم قتل (رضوان الله عليه).

Then Amr ibn Muta' al-Ju'fi joined the battle, chanting [verses declairing his intent to protect al-Hussain (a)]. He continued to fight until he killed thirty soldiers, then he was killed - may God bless his soul.[48]

# The Martyrdom of Anees ibn Ma'qil al-Asbahi

ثم خرج من بعده أنيس بن معقل الأصبحي، فجعل [يرتجز] ثم حمل و لم يزل
يقاتل حتى قتل [على رواية ابن شهر اشوب] نيّفا و عشرين رجلا، ثم قتل
(رضوان الله عليه).

Then Anees ibn Ma'qil al-Asbahi entered the battlefield. He cried out
[verses in praise of al-Hussain (a) that announced his dedication to the
protection of the Holy Household (a)]. He charged at the enemy and
fought until he killed twenty some men [according to Ibn
Shahrashoob] before he was killed - may God bless his soul.[49]

# The Martyrdom of al-Hajjaj ibn Masrouq al-Ju'fi

ثم برز من بعده الحجاج بن مسروق الجعفي، و هو مؤذّن الحسين (عليه
السلام)، و كان قد خرج من الكوفة إلى مكة فالتحق بالحسين (عليه السلام)،
و صحبه منها إلى العراق، فجعل [يرتجز] ثم حمل على القوم و قاتل قتال
المشتاقين، حتى قتل منهم ثمانية عشر رجلا، ثم قتل (رضوان الله عليه).

Then al-Hajjaj ibn Masrouq al-Ju'fi, who was al-Hussain's (a) *Muazzin*,[*]
set out into battle. He had left Kufa for Mecca, where he joined al-
Hussain (a) and came with him to Iraq. He [rushed into battle, chanting
verses in praise of the Holy Household (a)]. He charged and fought
like a man longing [for death]. He killed eighteen enemy men before
he was killed - may God bless his soul.[50]

---

[*] A *Muazzin* is an individual who recites the call to daily prayer at dawn, noon, and
dusk.

# Al-Hussain's (a) companions Enter the Battle in Groups

و لما نظر من بقي من أصحاب الحسين (عليه السلام) إلى كثرة من قتل منهم، أخذ الرجلان و الثلاثة و الأربعة يستأذنون الحسين (عليه السلام) في الذبّ عنه و الدفع عن حرمه، و كل واحد يحمي الآخر من كيد عدوه.

When the remainder of al-Hussain's (a) companions saw the many casualties of their camp, they began to approach in groups of two, three, and four, and seek permission to fight in his defense and the defense of his family. [They would enter the battlefield in groups] and each would protect the other from the charges of their enemies.[51]

# The Martyrdom of the Ghafari Brothers

فجاءه عبد الله و عبد الرحمن ابنا عروة [أو عزرة] الغفاريان، فقالا: يا أبا عبد

الله عليك السلام، قد حازنا الناس إليك، فأحببنا أن نقتل بين يديك (و ندفع

عنك). قال:

Then Abdullah and Abdulrahman, the sons of Urwa [or Uzra, as per some accounts] al-Ghafari, came to al-Hussain (a) and said, "Peace be upon you, O' Abu Abdullah. The people have grouped us with you, so we wish to be killed before you and in your defense." He said to them,

مرحبا بكما، ادنوا مني.

*Welcome! Come closer.*

فدنوا منه، و جعلا يقاتلان. و جعل عبد الرحمن يرتجز [...]فقاتل حتى قتل.

The drew closer to him and began to to fight, while Abdulrahman recited [verses taunting his enemies]. They fought until they were killed.[52]

# The Martyrdom of the Jabiri Brothers

و أتاه فتيان، و هما سيف بن الحارث بن سريع، و مالك بن عبد الله بن سريع الجابريان [في مقتل الخوارزمي: بطن من همدان يقال لهم بنو جابر]، و هما ابنا عم و أخوان لأم، و هما يبكيان. فقال لهما الحسين (عليه السلام):

Then two young men came to al-Hussain (a) crying. They were Saif ibn al-Harith ibn Saree' al-Jabiri and Malik ibn Abdullah ibn Saree' al-Jabiri [al-Khawarizmi says, "Banu Jabir are a branch of the Hamadan tribe"]. They were paternal cousins but brothers to the same mother [i.e. the father of one of them had married his brother's widow]. Al-Hussain (a) said to them,

يا ابني أخي، ما يبكيكما؟ فو الله إني لأرجو أن تكونا بعد (عن) ساعة قريري العين.

*O' sons of my brethren, why do you cry? By God, I only wish that you soon be well.*

فقالا: جعلنا الله فداك، و الله ما على أنفسنا نبكي، و لكن نبكي عليك، نراك و قد أحيط بك، و لا نقدر على أن ننفعك. فقال (عليه السلام):

They said, "May we be sacrificed for you! By God, we do not cry for ourselves, but rather for you. We see you surrounded but we cannot defend you." Al-Hussain (a) said,

جزاكما الله يا ابني أخي بوجدكما [أي حزنكما] من ذلك، و مواساتكما إياي بأنفسكما أحسن جزاء المتقين.

*May God reward you, O' sons of my brethren, for your sadness at this situation and your [sacrifice of your lives] with the best of rewards given to the pious.*

ثم استقدما و قالا: السلام عليك يابن رسول الله. فقال:

They stepped forward and said, "Peace be upon you, O' son of the Messenger of God (s)." He replied,

و عليكما السلام و رحمة الله و بركاته. فقاتلا حتى قتلا.

*May God's peace, mercy, and blessings be with you as well.*

# The Martyrdom of Junada ibn al-Harth al-Ansari

ثم خرج من بعده جنادة بن الحرث الأنصاري، و هو [يرتجز] فحمل و لم يزل
يقاتل حتى قتل ستة عشر رجلا، ثم قتل (رضوان الله عليه).

Then Junada ibn al-Harth al-Ansari stepped forward, reciting [verses in praise of his lineage]. He charged at the enemy and fought until he killed sixteen men before he was killed - may God bless his soul.[53]

# The Martyrdom of Amr ibn Junada al-Ansari

ثم خرج من بعده عمرو بن جنادة و هو [يرتجز] ثم حمل فقاتل حتى قتل.

Then Amr ibn Junada joined the battle reciting verses [decrying the wretchedness of his foes]. He charged at the enemy and fought until he was killed.[54]

# The Martyrdom of Wadih al-Turki Servant of al-Harth al-Mithhiji

كان (واضح) غلاما تركيا شجاعا قارئا، و هو مولى للحارث المذحجي السلماني. و قد أبلى في كربلاء بلاء حسنا. و لما صرع واضح التركي [أي سقط و به رمق]، استغاث بالحسين (عليه السلام)؛ فأتاه أبو عبد الله (عليه السلام) و اعتنقه و هو يجود بنفسه، فقال: من مثلي و ابن رسول الله (ص) واضع خدّه على خدي!. ثم فاضت نفسه الطاهرة.

Wadih was a young turkish man, a brave warrior, and a reciter [of the Holy Quran]. He was a servant of al-Harth al-Mithhiji al-Salmani. He made a valiant stand in the land of Karbala. When Wadih al-Turki was felled, he called al-Hussain (a) for help. Abu Abdullah (a) came to him and hugged him as he was taking his last breaths. Wadih said, "Who is like me when the son of the Messenger of God (a) has put his cheek on my cheek!" His holy soul then departed this world.[55]

# The Martyrdom of Abu Omar al-Nahshali

و حدّث مهران مولى بني كاهل، قال: شهدت كربلاء مع الحسين (عليه السلام) فرأيت رجلا يقاتل قتالا شديدا؛ لا يحمل على قوم إلا كشفهم، ثم يرجع إلى الحسين (عليه السلام) و هو يرتجز [...] فقلت: من هذا؟ فقالوا: أبو عمر النهشلي، و قيل الخثعمي. فاعترضه عامر بن نهشل، فقتله و احتزّ رأسه. و كان أبو عامر هذا متهجّدا كثير الصلاة.

Mahran the Servant of Banu Kahil said, "I witnessed Karbala alongside al-Hussain (a) and saw a man fighting valiantly. Whenever he charged at the enemy, he repelled them. Then he would return to al-Hussain (a), reciting [verses of encouragement and praise]. I asked, 'Who is this man?' They said, 'Abu Omar al-Nahhshali' or 'al-Khath'ami.' Then Amir ibn Nahshal fought him, killed him, and severed his head. Abu Omar used to spend the nights in worship and continuous prayers."[56]

# The Martyrdom of Aslam al-Turki the Servant of al-Hussain (a)

أنه كان للحسين (عليه السلام) مولى اسمه أسلم بن عمرو، و كان اشتراه بعد وفاة أخيه الحسن (عليه السلام)، و وهبه لابنه علي بن الحسين (عليه السلام). و كان أبوه (عمرو) تركيا. و كان (أسلم) هذا كاتبا عند الحسين (عليه السلام) في بعض حوائجه. لما خرج الحسين (عليه السلام) من المدينة إلى مكة كان أسلم ملازما له، حتى أتى معه كربلاء. فلما كان اليوم العاشر و شبّ القتال، استأذن في القتال.

Al-Hussain (a) had a servant names Aslam ibn Amr. He had bought him after the martyrdom of his brother al-Hassan (a) and gifted him to his son Ali ibn al-Hussain (a). His father, Amr, was turkish. Aslam was also a scribe for al-Hussain (a) in some instances. When al-Hussain (a) left Medina towards Mecca, Aslam accompanied him and was with him until they reached Karbala. On the tenth of Muharram when the battle commenced, Aslam sought permission to fight.]

و خرج غلام تركي من موالي الحسين (عليه السلام)، و كان قارئا للقرآن و عارفا بالعربية و كاتبا، فجعل يقاتل و يرتجز [...]فقتل [في رواية ابن شهر اشوب] سبعين رجلا، فتحاوشوه حتى سقط صريعا، فجاء إليه الحسين (عليه السلام) فبكى، و وضع خده على خده، ففتح عينيه فرأى الحسين (عليه السلام) فتبسم، ثم صار إلى ربه.

A turkish servant of al-Hussain (a) set out for battle, and he was a reciter of the Quran, had knowledge of the Arabic language, and was also a scribe. He fought as he recited [verses taunting his enemies]. He killed seventy men [according to Ibn Shahrashoob] before he was surrounded and felled. Al-Hussain (a) came to him, wept, and placed his cheek over Aslam's cheek. Aslam opened his eyes and saw al-Hussain (a). He smiled and his soul departed this world to the next.[57]

# The Martyrdom of Malik ibn Thawdan

ثم برز مالك بن ذودان [وهو يرتجز] فقاتل حتى قتل (رضوان الله عليه).

Then Malik ibn Thawdan joined the battle, reciting [verses that declared his might and his intent to protect the family of the Prophet (s)]. He fought until he was killed, may God bless his soul.[58]

# The Martyrdom of Ibrahim ibn al-Hossayn al-Asadi

و برز إبراهيم بن الحصين الأسدي و هو يرتجز [...]فقتل [على رواية ابن شهر اشوب] أربعة و ثمانين رجلا [...]و قاتل حتى قتل (رضوان الله عليه).

Ibrahim ibn al-Hossayn set out for the battlefield, [taunting his enemies with a poetic battle cry]. He killed eighty four men [according to Ibn Shahrashoob] and began to recite [verses of poetry in praise of al-Hussain (a) and his noble lineage]. He fought until he was killed - may God bless his soul.[59]

# The Martyrdom of Sawwar al-Fahmi al-Hamadani

و قاتل سوّار بن أبي عمير من ولد فهم بن جابر الهمداني، قاتلا شديدا حتى ارتثّ بالجراح و أخذ أسيرا، فأراد ابن سعد قتله، و تشفّع فيه قومه، و بقي عندهم جريحا إلى أن توفي على رأس ستة أشهر، (رحمه الله).

Sawwar ibn Abu Omair, a descendent of Fahm ibn Jabir al-Hamadani, joined the battle and fought until he was overburdened by his wounds and taken as a captive. Omar ibn Saad wanted to kill him, but his kin interceded for him. He remained with them a wounded prisoner until he died after six months - may God bless his soul.[60]

# The Martyrdom of Saad ibn al-Harith and his Brother Abu al-Hutuf

و لما سمع الأنصاريان: سعد بن الحارث و أخوه أبو الحتوف، استنصار الحسين
(عليه السلام) و استغاثته، و كانا في جيش عمر بن سعد، فمالا بسيفيهما على
أعداء الحسين، و قاتلا حتى قتلا.

Saad ibn al-Harith al-Ansari and his brother Abu al-Hutuf heard the
calls of al-Hussain (a) for aid and support while they were in the army
of Omar ibn Saad. They took their swords and charged at the enemies
of al-Hussain (a), and fought until they were killed.

# The Martyrdom of Sowaid ibn Amr ibn Abu Muta' al-Khath'ami

و أما سويد بن أبي المطاع فكان قد صرع، فوقع بين القتلى مثخنا بالجراحات
(و ظنّ أنه قتل). فلما قتل الحسين (عليه السلام) و سمعهم يقولون: قتل الحسين
(عليه السلام)، فوجد خفّة، فتحامل و أخرج سكّينة من خفّه (و كان سيفه
قد أخذ)، فقاتلهم بسكينه ساعة. و كان يرتجز [...]و تعطّفوا عليه فقتلوه. قتله
عروة بن بطان الثعلبي و زيد بن رقّاد الجبني. و كان سويد آخر من قتل من
أصحاب الحسين (عليه السلام).

As for Sowaid ibn Abi al-Muta', he had been felled and left wounded amongst the dead. When al-Hussain (a) was killed and he heard the enemy cry out the news, he reached into his satchel and grabbed a knife [his sword had been taken]. He stood and fought the enemy for some time, reciting [verses in praise of al-Hussain (a) and his noble lineage]. The enemy charged at him and finished him off. He was killed by Urwa ibn Bitan al-Tha'labi and Zaid ibn Raqqad al-Jubni. Sowaid was the last martyr of the companions of al-Hussain (a).

# Every Individual Killed in the Way of God is a Martyr

و كان يأتي الحسين الرجل بعد الرجل، فيقول: السلام عليك يابن رسول اللّه،
فيجيبه الحسين (عليه السلام):

One by one, the companions would come to al-Hussain (a) and say, "Peace be upon you, O' son of the Messenger of God (s)." He would reply,

و عليك السلام، و نحن خلفك، فَمِنْهُمْ مَنْ قَضَى نَحْبَهُ وَ مِنْهُمْ مَنْ
يَنْتَظِرُ [الأحزاب: 23]

*Peace be upon you. We will soon follow you. 'There are some among them who have fulfilled their pledge, and some of them who still wait' (The Holy Quran 33:23).*

ثم يحمل فيقتل. حتى قتلوا عن آخرهم (رضوان الله عليهم)، و لم يبق مع الحسين
(عليه السلام) إلا أهل بيته. (يقول الخوارزمي): و هكذا يكون المؤمن، يؤثر
دينه على دنياه، و موته على حياته، في سبيل اللّه، ينصر الحق و إن قتل. قال
تعالى:

Each would charge at the enemy and fight until he is killed. Every single one of the companions was killed - may God bless their souls - and no one remained with al-Hussain (a) but his family members. Al-Khawarizmi says: This is how a believer should be; preferring his faith over his material gains and his death over his life, all for the sake of God. He should support the truth, even if he is to be killed. God Almighty says,

وَ لَا تَحْسَبَنَّ الَّذِينَ قُتِلُوا فِي سَبِيلِ اللهِ أَمْوَاتاً بَلْ أَحْيَاءٌ عِنْدَ رَبِّهِمْ يُرْزَقُونَ [آل عمران: 169].

*Do not suppose those who were slain in the way of God to be dead; no, they are living and provided for near their Lord.*

و قال النبي (صلى الله عليه و آله و سلم):

The Prophet (s) said,

كل قتيل في جنب الله شهيد.

*Every individual killed in the way of God is a martyr.*

و لما وقف رسول اللّه (صلى الله عليه و آله و سلم) على شهداء أحد و فيهم حمزة بن عبد المطلب، قال:

When the Messenger of God (s) stood over the martyrs of Uhud, and amongst them was Hamza ibn Abdulmuttalib, he said,

أنا شهيد هؤلاء القوم، زمّلوهم بدمائهم، فإنهم يحشرون يوم القيامة و كلومهم رواء، و أوداجهم تشخب دما؛ فاللون لون الدم، و الريح ريح المسك.

*I am the witness over these people. Wrap them in their [bloodied garments]. They will be revived on the Day of Resurrection with their wounds pouring and their [severed] veins streaming with blood. It's color will be the color of blood, but its odor will be the aroma of musk.[61]*

# The Martyrdom of Ahlulbayt

# The Martyrs of the Holy Household

و لما قتل أصحاب الحسين (عليه السلام)، و لم يبق إلا أهل بيته، و هم: ولد

علي (عليه السلام)، و ولد جعفر، و ولد عقيل، و ولد الحسن، و ولده (عليه

السلام)، و عددهم على الأشهر 17 شخصا، اجتمعوا و ودّع بعضهم بعضا و

عزموا على الحرب.

When the companions of Al-Hussain (a) were slain, none but his household remained. They were the sons of Ali [ibn abi Talib] (a), the sons of Jafar [ibn Abi Talib], the sons of 'Aqil [ibn Abi Talib], the sons of Al-Hassan [ibn Ali ibn Abi Talib] (a), and his own [Imam Hussain's (a)] sons. They numbered 17 individuals, as is most widely believed. They gathered and said their farewells, preparing themselves for battle.[62]

# Ali Al-Akbar (a) Sets Out for the Battlefield

و أول من تقدّم إلى البراز علي الأكبر (عليه السلام) و عمره سبع و عشرون

سنة فإنه ولد في 11 شعبان سنة 33 هـ. و أمه ليلى بنت أبي مرة بن عروة

بن مسعود الثقفي.

The first of them to step forward was Ali Al-Akbar who was 27 years old (born on 11 Sha'ban, 33 AH). His mother was Layla bint Abi Murra ibn Orwa ibn Masood Al-Thaqafi.[63]

# The Martyrdom of Ali Al-Akbar

فاستأذن أباه في القتال، فأذن له. ثم نظر إليه نظرة آيس منه، و أرخى عينيه فبكى. ثم رفع سبابتيه نحو السماء و قال:

[Ali Al-Akbar] took permission from his father to set out for battle and he was granted permission. [Imam Hussain (a)] looked at him with desperation and began to cry. He raised his index finger to the sky and said,

اللّهم كن أنت الشهيد عليهم، فقد برز إليهم غلام أشبه الناس خلقا و خلقا و منطقا برسولك محمّد (صلى الله عليه و آله و سلم) و كنا إذا اشتقنا إلى وجه رسولك نظرنا إلى وجهه. اللّهم فامنعهم بركات الأرض، و إن منعتهم ففرقهم تفريقا، و مزّقهم تمزيقا، و اجعلهم طرائق قددا، و لا ترض الولاة عنهم أبدا. فإنهم دعونا لينصرونا، ثم عدوا علينا يقاتلونا و يقتلونا.

*My God, be witness to [their deeds], for a young man has come forward to them who is most like Your Messenger Muhammad (s) in his countenance, morals, and demeanor. Whenever we missed the countenance of Your Messenger (s), we would look towards [Ali Al-Akbar]. My God, deprive them of the blessings of the earth, and after you have deprived them so divide them into factions, tear them apart, make them into various sects, and do not ever let their governors be pleased with them! They invited us with the promise that they would aid us, but they have turned against us, fighting and killing us!*

ثم صاح الحسين (عليه السلام) بعمر بن سعد:

Al-Hussain (a) then cried out to Omar ibn Saad,

مالك قطع الله رحمك و لا بارك لك في أمرك، و سلّط عليك من يذبحك على فراشك، كما قطعت رحمي و لم تحفظ قرابتي من رسول الله (صلى الله عليه و آله و سلم.

*What is wrong with you? May God sever your lineage and never bless you in any matter! [May God] empower over you one who would slay you on you bed! This is just as you have severed my lineage and did not respect my kinship to the Messenger of God (s).*

ثم رفع صوته و قرأ:

He then raised his voice in recitation,

إنَّ اللَّهَ اضْطَفَى آدَمَ وَ نُوحاً وَ آلَ إِبْراهِيمَ وَ آلَ عِمْرانَ عَلَى الْعالَمِينَ، ذُرِّيَّةً بَعْضُها مِنْ بَعْضٍ وَ اللَّهُ سَمِيعٌ عَلِيمٌ. [آل عمران: 33- 34]

*Indeed God chose Adam and Noah, and the progeny of Abraham and the progeny of Imran above all the nations; some of them are descendants of the others, and God is all-hearing, all-knowing. (The Holy Quran, 3:33-34)*

ثم حمل علي بن الحسين (عليه السلام) و هو يقول:

Ali Al-Akbar then charged while reciting in verse,

أنا علي بن الحسين بن علي * * * نحن و بيت الله أولى بالنبي

و الله لا يحكم فينا ابن الدّعي * * * أطعنكم بالرمح حتى ينثني

أضربكم بالسيف حتى يلتوي * * * ضرب غلام هاشميّ علوي

*I am Ali ibn Al-Hussain ibn Ali (a)*

119

*We are, by the House of God, more worthy of the Prophet [and his example]*

*By God, the son of the imposter will not rule over us*

*I will stab you with the spear until it breaks*

*I will strike you with the sword until it bends*

*The strikes of a young Hashemite, Alid man.*

و كان علي الأكبر (عليه السلام) مرآة الجمال النبوي، و مثال خلقه السامي، و أنموذجا من منطقه البليغ [...] و في (الدمعة الساكبة): لما توجّه علي الأكبر إلى الحرب، اجتمعت النساء حوله كالحلقة، و قلن له: ارحم غربتنا، و لا تستعجل إلى القتال، فإنه ليس لنا طاقة في فراقك. قال: فلم يزل يجهد و يبالغ في طلب الإذن من أبيه، حتى أذن له. ثم ودّع أباه و الحرم، و توجّه نحو الميدان.

Ali Al-Akbar was a reflection of prophetic beauty, an example of [the Prophet's (s) teachings in] high morals, and a likeness of the [Prophet's (s)] eloquent speech. [...] In *Al-Dam'a Al-Sakiba* [by Al-Waheed Al-Behbahani] it says: When Ali Al-Akbar head towards battle, the women gathered around him in a circle and said, "Have mercy on our forsakenness and do not rush to battle, for we do not have the power to overcome your loss." He continued to ask for permission from his father until he was granted permission. He bade farewell to his father and the women and headed towards the battlefield.

فلم يزل يقاتل حتى ضجّ أهل الكوفة لكثرة من قتل منهم، حتى أنه روي أنه على عطشه قتل 120 رجلا. ثم رجع إلى أبيه الحسين (عليه السلام) و قد أصابته جراحات كثيرة. فقال: يا أبت العطش قد قتلني، و ثقل الحديد قد أجهدني،

فهل إلى شربة من ماء سبيل، أتقوى بها على الأعداء؟. فبكى الحسين (عليه السلام) و قال:

He continued to fight until the Kufans became distraught by the amount of them he had killed. It is even narrated that he had killed, despite his thirst, 120 men. He then returned to his father, having been severely injured, and said, "O' father, thirst is killing me and the weight of iron has tired me. Is there means by which I can get a sip of water to strengthen me against my enemies?" Al-Hussain (a) wept and said,

يا بنيّ عزّ على محمّد و على علي و على أبيك، أن تدعوهم فلا يجيبوك، و تستغيث بهم فلا يغيثوك.

*My son, it saddens Muhammad (s), Ali (a), and your father that you call them but they do not answer you and that you plead for their aid but they do not aid you. [...]*

و دفع إليه خاتمه و قال له

[Imam Hussain (a)] then gave him his ring and said,

خذ هذا الخاتم في فيك، و ارجع إلى قتال عدوك، فإني أرجو أن لا تمسي حتى يسقيك جدك بكأسه الأوفى شربة لا تظمأ بعدها أبدا.

*Put this ring in your mouth and return to battle against your enemy. Surely, I hope that night does not fall before your grandfather gives you out of his overflowing cup a drink after which you will never thirst.*

و من جهة أن ليلى أم علي الأكبر هي بنت ميمونة ابنة أبي سفيان صاح رجل من القوم: يا علي إن لك رحما بأمير المؤمنين [يزيد] و نريد أن نرعى الرحم، فإن شئت آمنّاك!. فقال (عليه السلام): إن قرابة رسول الله أحقّ أن ترعى.

Because Layla, Ali Al-Akbar's mother, was the daughter of Maymouna bint Abi Sufyan, a man called out, "O' Ali, you have a blood relation to the Prince of the Believers [Yazid], and we wish to respect that blood relation. If you wish, we will grant you sanctuary!" He replied, "Surely, the blood relation to the Messenger of God (s) is more worthy of being respected."

فرجع علي بن الحسين إلى القتال [...]و جعل يقاتل حتى قتل تمام المئتين (و في رواية: فقال مرّة بن منقذ العبدي: عليّ آثام العرب إن لم أثكل أباه به، فطعنه بالرمح في ظهره). ثم ضربه (مرّة) على مفرق رأسه ضربة صرعه فيها، و ضربه الناس بأسيافهم، فاعتنق الفرس فحمله الفرس إلى عسكر عدوه، فقطّعوه بأسيافهم إربا إربا.

He then returned to battle. [...] He continued to fight until he killed an even 200. [One narration states that Murra ibn Munqith Al-Abdi said, 'May I bear all the sins of the Arabs if I do not bereave his father by killing him.' He then struck [Ali Al-Akbar] with a spear in his back.] Then Murra struck him on the top of his head, felling him. Men continued to strike him with their swords, so he held on to [the neck of] the horse which carried him into the enemy camp. They tore him to pieces with their swords.

فلما بلغت روحه التراقي نادى بأعلى صوته: يا أبتاه! هذا جدي رسول الله قد سقاني بكأسه الأوفى شربة لا أظمأ بعدها أبدا، و هو يقول لك: العجل، فإن لك كأسا مذخورة. فصاح الحسين (عليه السلام):

When his soul was about to leave his body he called at the top of his voice, "O' father, here is my grandfather, the Messenger of God (s), giving me a drink out of his overflowing cup, after which I shall never

thirst. He says to you, 'Make haste, for there is a cup waiting for you.'"
Al-Hussain (a) called out,

قتل الله قوما قتلوك يا بني، ما أجرأهم على الله و على انتهاك حرمة
رسول الله، على الدنيا بعدك العفا.

*May God kill a people which have killed you, my son. What audacity
do they have against God in desecrating the sanctity of the Messenger of
God (s)! The world may just as well end after you!*

و روي أن الحسين (عليه السلام) بكى عليه بكاء شديدا. و في (ناسخ التواريخ)
أن الحسين (عليه السلام) لما جاء إلى ولده، رآه و به رمق، و فتح علي (عليه
السلام) عينيه في وجه أبيه، و قال: يا أبتاه أرى أبواب السماء قد انفتحت، و
الحور العين بيدها كؤوس الماء قد نزلن من السماء، و هن يدعونني إلى الجنة؛
فأوصيك بهذه النسوة، بأن لا يخمشن عليّ وجها. ثم سكن و انقطع أنينه.

It is narrated that Al-Hussain (a) wept heavily for his loss. In *Nasikh
Al-Tawareekh* it is relayed that Al-Hussain (a) reached his son while he
still had a breath in him. Ali [Al-Akbar] opened his eyes and said,
"Father, I see the doors of the heavens open and the servants of
heaven are descending with cups of water, calling me to paradise. I ask
you to instruct the women not to scratch their faces in mourning me."
He then became still and his voice became quiet.

و في (الفاجعة العظمى) ص 137، قال أبو مخنف: و وضع الحسين (عليه
السلام) رأس ولده علي في حجره، و جعل يمسح الدم عن ثناياه، و جعل يلثمه
و يقول:

In *Al-Faji'a Al-'Othma* Abu Mikhnaf writes: Al-Hussain (a) put his son's head on his lap and wiped the blood off his mouth. He would kiss him and say,

يا بني، لعن الله قوما قتلوك، ما أجرأهم على الله و رسوله (صلى الله عليه و آله و سلم).

*My son, may God curse a people who would kill you. What audacity do they have against God and His Messenger (s)!*

و هملت عيناه بالدموع و قال:

His eyes drowned in tears as he said,

أما أنت يا بني، فقد استرحت من كرب الدنيا و محنها، و صرت إلى روح و ريحان، و بقي أبوك، و ما أسرع لحوقه بك.

*My son, you have gained comfort from the troubles and tribulations of the world, and have reached a place of ease and abundance. Your father remains, but will surely follow you soon.*

قال: و جعل الحسين (عليه السلام) يتنفس الصعداء. و في (المنتخب): و صاح الحسين (عليه السلام) بأعلى صوته، فتصارخن النساء. و قال لهن الحسين (عليه السلام):

Al-Hussain (a) would take deep, heavy breaths. In *Al-Muntakhab*: Al-Hussain (a) cried at the top of his voice and the women began to weep. He said to them,

اسكتن، فإن البكاء أمامكنّ.

*Settle down, there will be much weeping ahead.*[64]

# Lady Zaynab Mourns Ali Al-Akbar

و روي أن زينب (عليها السلام) خرجت مسرعة تنادي بالويل و الثبور، و
تقول: يا حبيباه. قال حميد بن مسلم: لكأني أنظر إلى امرأة خرجت مسرعة كأنها
شمس طالعة، تنادي بالويل و الثبور. تصيح: وا حبيباه! وا ثمرة فؤاداه! وا نور
عيناه! فسألت عنها، فقيل: هي زينب بنت علي (عليها السلام). ثم جاءت حتى
انكبّت عليه. فجاء إليها الحسين (عليه السلام) حتى أخذ بيدها و ردّها إلى
الفسطاط .. ثم أقبل مع فتيانه إلى ابنه، فقال:

It is narrated that Zaynab came out in a rush, warning of ill-fate and
destruction and calling "O' my beloved [nephew]." Hameed ibn
Muslim said, "I saw a woman rushing out. She appeared like the rising
sun and was warning of ill-fate and destruction while calling, 'O' my
beloved [nephew]! O' apple of my heart! O' light of my eye!' I asked
about her and was told, 'She is Zaynab bint Ali (a).' She continued until
she collapsed beside him. Al-Hussain (a) then came to her, took her by
the hand, and returned her to the tent. He came back to his son along
with the young men from his camp and said,

احملوا أخاكم.

*Carry your brother.*

فحملوه من مصرعه حتى وضعوه عند الفسطاط الّذي يقاتلون أمامه. و ذكر
الميانجي في (العيون العبرى) ص 153: و في الزيارة المروية عن الصادق (عليه
السلام):

They carried him back and placed him before the tent [...]." Al-Mayaniji
wrote in *al-Oyoon al-'Abra*: And in the visitation narrated from Al-Sadiq
(a),

بأبي أنت و أمي من مذبوح مقتول من غير جرم، و بأبي أنت و أمي
دمك المرتقى به إلى حبيب الله [أي النبي (صلى الله عليه و آله و
سلم)]، و بأبي أنت و أمي من مقدّم بين يدي أبيك يحتسبك و يبكي
عليك، محترقا عليك قلبه، يرفع دمك بكفّه إلى أعنان السماء، لا ترجع
منه قطرة، و لا تسكن من أبيك زفرة.

*May my father and mother be sacrificed for you, O' you who were slaughtered without a crime. May my father and mother be sacrificed for you, O' you whose blood was raised to God's Beloved [Prophet (s)]. May my father and mother be sacrificed for you, O' you who laid at his father's hands, grieving and weeping over you while his heart burns for you. He would raise your blood in his hands to the highest of the heavens and not a drop of it would return, while his heavy breaths never calm.[65]*

# The Martyrdom of Abdullah ibn Muslim ibn Aqeel

و برز عبد الله بن مسلم بن عقيل بن أبي طالب (عليه السلام)، و أمه رقية بنت علي (عليها السلام) [...] فقتل ثلاثة رجال فرماه عمرو بن صبيح الصيداوي [و في رواية: الصدائي] بسهم، فوضع عبد الله بن مسلم يده على جبهته يتّقيه، فأصاب السهم كفّه و نفذ إلى جبهته فسمّرها فلم يستطع أن يحرّكها. ثم طعنه أسيد بن مالك بالرمح في قلبه فقتله.

Abdullah ibn Muslim ibn Aqeel, whose mother was Ruqaya bint Ali (a), set out for the battlefield [...]. He killed three men but then was struck by the arrow of Amr ibn Subayh al-Saydawi. Abdullah lifted his hand to his forehead to guard against the arrow, but it pierced through his palm and reached his forehead. His hand was pinned to his forehead and he could not move it. Osaid ibn Malik then struck him with a spear in his chest, killing him.

(و قيل) إن قاتل عبد الله بن مسلم هو يزيد بن الرّقاد الجهني، و كان يقول: رميته بسهم و كفّه على جبهته يتقي النبل، فأثبتّ كفّه في جبهته، فما استطاع أن يزيل كفه عن جبهته. و قال حين رميته: اللّهم إنهم استقلّونا و استذلّونا، فاقتلهم كما قتلونا. ثم رماه بسهم آخر، و كان يقول: جئته و هو ميّت، فنزعت سهمي من جوفه، و لم أزل أنضنض الآخر عن جبهته حتى أخذته و بقي النصل.

It is also said that the killer of Abdullah ibn Muslim was Yazid ibn al-Raqqad al-Juhani. [Yazid] would say, "I shot him with an arrow while his hand was in front of his forehead guarding against the arrows. I pinned his hand to his forehead so that he could not move it. He said when I shot him so, 'O' God, they have isolated and subdued us, so kill them just as they killed us!'" [Yazid] then struck him with another arrow and would say afterwards, "I came to him after he had died and removed my arrow from his body. I continued to tug at the other arrow to remove it from his forehead until it separated and the arrowhead remained."[66]

# The Martyrdom of Muhammad ibn Muslim ibn Aqeel

و خرج محمّد بن مسلم بن عقيل بن أبي طالب (عليه السلام)، فقاتل حتى
قتل. قتله أبو جرهم الأزدي و لقيط بن ياسر الجهني.

Then Muhammad ibn Muslim ibn Aqeel set out for the battlefield and fought until he was felled. His killers were Abu Jarham al-Azdi and Laqeet ibn Yasir al-Juhani.[67]

# The Martyrdom of the Remainder of the Hashemites

و لما قتل عبد الله بن مسلم، حمل آل أبي طالب حملة واحدة. فصاح بهم الحسين (عليه السلام):

And when Abdullah ibn Muslim ibn Aqeel was killed, the family of Abu Talib set out onto the battle field in a single push. Al-Hussain (a) called out to them,

صبرا على الموت يا بني عمومتي، و الله لا رأيتم هوانا بعد هذا اليوم أبدا.

*Be patient in the face of death, O' cousins. By God, you will never experience meekness after this day.*[68]

# The Martyrdom of Some of the Sons of Aqeel

فخرج جعفر بن عقيل بن أبي طالب (عليه السلام)، فحمل [...] فقتل خمسة عشر فارسا [على رواية محمّد بن أبي طالب]، و راجلين [على رواية ابن شهر اشوب]. فقتله عبد اللّه بن عروة الخثعمي، و قيل بشر بن سوط الهمداني.

Then Jafar ibn Aqeel ibn Abi Talib stepped forward unto the battlefield [...] killing 15 cavalrymen [according to the historical account of Muhammad ibn Abi Talib] and 2 infantrymen [according to ibn Shahrashoob]. He was killed by Abdullah ibn Orwa al-Khath'ami, or [as in other historical accounts] Bishr ibn Sawt al-Hamadani.

ثم خرج من بعده أخوه عبد الرحمن بن عقيل، فحمل [...] فقتل [على رواية محمّد بن أبي طالب و ابن شهر اشوب] سبعة عشر فارسا. فحمل عليه عثمان بن خالد الجهني و بشر بن سوط الهمداني فقتلاه.

He was followed by his brother Abdulrahman ibn Aqeel [...] who killed seventeen cavalrymen [according to both Muhammad ibn Abi Talib and Ibn Shahrashoob]. He was attacked and killed by Othman ibn Khalid al-Juhani and Bishr ibn Sawt al-Hamadani.

و خرج عبد اللّه الأكبر بن عقيل بن أبي طالب (عليه السلام) فما زال يضرب فيهم حتى أثخن بالجراح و سقط إلى الأرض. فجاء عثمان بن خالد التميمي و بشر بن سوط فقتلاه.

Then Abdullah the Elder ibn Aqeel ibn Abi Talib set out for the battlefield. He continued to fight until he was severely wounded and fell to the ground. Othman ibn Khalid al-Tamimi and Bishr ibn Sawt came to him and finished him off.

و أصابت الحسن المثنّى ابن الإمام الحسن (عليه السلام) ثماني عشرة جراحة و قطعت يده اليمنى، و لم يستشهد. ثم برز من بعده موسى بن عقيل (عليه السلام) [....] ثم حمل على القوم و لم يزل يقاتل حتى قتل سبعين فارسا، ثم قتل (رحمه الله).

[Amongst the sons of Aqeel was] al-Hassan II, the son of Imam Hassan (a), who was wounded and his right hand was severed, but he was not martyred. Musa ibn Aqeel then set out to the battle field [...] and was charged by the enemies. He continued to fight until he killed 70 cavalrymen, but was eventually killed.[69]

# The Martyrdom of Ibrahim ibn Al-Hussain (a)

و برز من بعده إبراهيم بن الحسين، و هو [يرتجز] ثم حمل على القوم فقتل
خمسين فارسا، و قتل (رحمه الله).

Then Ibrahim ibn Al-Hussain (a) stepped forward unto the battlefield
[reciting verses of poetry written in honor of his father.] He charged
the enemies, killing fifty cavalrymen before being killed - may God
have mercy on his soul.[70]

# The Martyrdom of Ahmad ibn Muhammad al-Hashemi

و برز من بعده أحمد بن محمد الهاشمي، و هو يرتجز [...] ثم حمل على القوم، و لم يزل يقاتل حتى قتل ثمانين فارسا، ثم قتل (رضوان الله عليه).

Then Ahmad ibn Muhammad al-Hashemi stepped forward, [declaring in verse his intent to defend Imam Hussain (a).] He charged the enemy and fought valiantly until he killed eighty cavalrymen before being killed - may God be pleased with him.[71]

# Martyrdom of Muhammad and Aoun, the Sons of Abdullah ibn Jafar

و حمل الناس على الحسين (عليه السلام) و أهل بيته من كل جانب. فخرج محمّد بن عبد اللّه بن جعفر بن أبي طالب (عليه السلام)، و أمه زينب الكبرى بنت أمير المؤمنين (عليه السلام)، و قيل الخوصاء من بني تيم اللات، و هو [يرتجز] ثم قاتل حتى قتل عشرة أنفس، فحمل عليه عامر بن نهشل التميمي فقتله.

The enemies attacked al-Hussain (a) and his household from every direction. Muhammad ibn Abdullah ibn Jafar ibn Abi Talib stepped forward. His mother was [Lady] Zaynab, the daughter of the Commander of the Faithful (a), or according to some sources al-Khawsa', a woman from the tribe of Taim al-Laat. [He declared in verse his contempt for an enemy that had abandoned the teachings of the Holy Quran.] He fought and killed ten enemies, but was attacked and killed by 'Amir ibn Nahshal al-Tamimi.

و خرج أخوه عون بن عبد اللّه بن جعفر (عليه السلام) و أمه زينب الكبرى (عليها السلام) و هو [يرتجز] ثم قاتل حتى قتل [على رواية ابن شهر اشوب] ثلاثة فوارس و ثمانية عشر راجلا. فحمل عليه عبد اللّه بن قطبة الطائي فقتله.

His brother Aoun ibn Abdullah ibn Jafar then set out, and his mother was [Lady] Zaynab. He [stepped onto the battlefielding declaring his lineage and praising his father in verse.] He fought and killed [according to the account of Ibn Shahrashoob] three cavalrymen and eighteen infintrymen. He was attacked by Abdullah ibn Qutba al-Taei and killed.[72]

# The Martyrdom of Abdullah al-Akbar ibn al-Hassan (a)

و خرج أبو بكر بن الحسن (عليه السلام) و هو عبد الله الأكبر، و أمه أم ولد يقال لها رملة، و هي أم القاسم (عليه السلام)، برز [وهو يرتجز] فقاتل حتى قتل. و كان عبد الله بن الحسن (عليه السلام) قد تزوج من ابنة عمه سكينة بنت الحسين (عليه السلام) قبيل المعركة [...].

[Abdullah al-Akbar] ibn al-Hassan (a), [whose mother was Ramla] the mother of al-Qasim, set out unto the battlefield [reciting battle verses adapted from the poetry of his grandfather the Commander of the Faithful (a).] He fought until he was slain. He had been recently married to his cousin Sukayna bint al-Hussain (a) [at the time of the Battle of Karbala].[73]

# The Martyrdom of al-Qasim ibn al-Hassan (a)

و خرج من بعده أخوه لأمه و أبيه القاسم بن الحسن (عليه السلام)، و أمه أم
ولد، و هو غلام لم يبلغ الحلم. فلما نظر الحسين (عليه السلام) إليه قد برز،
اعتنقه و جعلا يبكيان حتى غشي عليهما. ثم استأذن عمه في المبارزة فأبى أن
يأذن له، فلم يزل الغلام يقبّل يديه و رجليه، حتى أذن له. فخرج و دموعه
تسيل على خديه و هو يقول:

[After the martyrdom of Abdullah al-Akbar ibn al-Hassan (a)], his full
brother al-Qasim ibn al-Hassan (a) came forward... and he had not yet
reached the age of adolescence. When al-Hussain saw him come
forward he embraced him and they wept until they fainted. [Al-Qasim]
asked his uncle for permission to enter the battlefield but his request
was denied. He continued to [beg his uncle for permission] kissing his
hands and feet, until he was granted permission. [Al-Qasim] stepped
forward unto the battlefield with tears running down his cheeks as he
said [in verse],

إن تنكروني فأنا ابن الحسن * * * سبط النبي المصطفى و المؤتمن
هذا حسين كالأسير المرتهن * * * بين أناس لا سقوا صوب المزن

*If you do not know me, I am the son of al-Hassan (a)*

*The grandson of the Chosen and Trusted Prophet (s)*

*And this is Hussain (a) like a ransomed captive*

*Amongst a [cursed] people; may the sky never rain its mercy upon them!*

فقاتل قتالا شديدا، حتى قتل على صغر سنّه [على بعض الروايات] خمسة و
ثلاثين رجلا.

ثم إن القاسم تقدم إلى عمر بن سعد، و قال له: يا عمر أما تخاف الله، أما تراقب الله يا أعمى القلب، أما تراعي رسول الله (صلى الله عليه و آله و سلم)؟! فقال عمر: أما كفاكم التجبر، أما تطيعون يزيد؟ فقال القاسم (عليه السلام): لا جزاك الله خيرا، تدّعي الإسلام، و آل رسول الله (صلى الله عليه و آله و سلم) عطاشى ظماء، قد اسودّت الدنيا بأعينهم.

He fought valiantly until he killed [according to some accounts] thirty five men.

Al-Qasim approached Omar ibn Saad and said, 'O' Omar, do you not fear God? Has your heart been so blinded that you do not heed [God's wrath]? Do you not take account of [the rights of] the Messenger of God (s)?" Omar replied, "Enough with your pride! Why do you not obey Yazid?" Al-Qasim said, "May God not reward you for any deed! You claim Islam while the household of the Messenger of God (s) are thirsty and the world grows dark in their eyes!"

قال حميد بن مسلم: كنت في عسكر ابن سعد، حين خرج علينا غلام كأن وجهه شقة قمر، و في يده سيف، و عليه قميص و إزار و نعلان، قد انقطع شسع إحداهما، ما أنسى أنها كانت اليسرى [و أنف ابن النبي (صلى الله عليه و آله و سلم) أن يحتفي في الميدان، فوقف يشدّ شسع نعله] [...].

Hamid ibn Muslim says: I was in the camp of [Omar] ibn Saad when a young man came forward whose face was like the shining moon. He carried a sword... and the strap of one shoe was torn - I will never forget that it was the left. [Al-Qasim refused to walk bearfoot in battle, as that was seen to be disgraceful. He stopped in the middle of the battlefield and knelt down to fix his shoe.] [...]

فقال لي عمرو بن سعد بن نفيل الأزدي: و الله لأشدّنّ عليه. فقلت: سبحان الله و ما تريد بذلك! و الله لو ضربني ما بسطت إليه يدي، دعه يكفيكه هؤلاء الذين تراهم قد احتوشوه. فقال: و الله لأفعلنّ. فشدّ عليه، فما ولّى حتى ضرب رأسه بالسيف ففلقه، و وقع الغلام إلى الأرض لوجهه، و نادى: يا عمّاه!

Amr ibn Saad ibn Nufayl al-Azdi said to me, 'By God, I shall assault him!' I said, 'Glory be to God! What do you hope to achieve by this! By God, if he were to strike me I would not extend my hand [to strike him back]. Leave him, for those who have gathered around him will be enough. He replied, 'By God, I will do [as I have said].' He charged toward [al-Qasim] and did not stop until he struck him on his head with the sword, cutting it in half. The young man fell on his face and called, 'O' uncle.'

فانقضّ عليه الحسين (عليه السلام) كالصقر، و تخلل الصفوف، و شدّ شدة ليث أغضب، فضرب عمرو بن سعد بن نفيل بالسيف، فاتقاها بالساعد فقطعها من لدن المرفق، فصاح صيحة سمعها أهل العسكر. ثم تنحّى عنه الحسين (عليه السلام) فحملت خيل أهل الكوفة ليستنقذوه، فاستقبلته بصدورها و وطئته بحوافرها، فمات.

Al-Hussain (a) charged toward him like a falcon, tearing through [enemy] lines like a angered lion. He struck Amr ibn Saad ibn Nufayl with the sword. [Amr] guarded against the blow with his forearm, leaving his arm severed at the elbow. He cried out so that the entire camp could hear him. Al-Hussain (a) moved back away from him while the Kufan cavalry approached, trying to save [Amr]. But as the cavalry charged, the horses hit him with their chests and trampled him under their feet, killing him.

و انجلت الغبرة فإذا بالحسين (عليه السلام) قائم على رأس الغلام و هو يفحص برجليه، و الحسين (عليه السلام) يقول:

When the dust settled, al-Hussain (a) was standing over the boy's head while he was digging with his feet [out of pain]. Al-Hussain (a) would say,

بُعدا لقوم قتلوك و من خصمهم يوم القيامة فيك جدك و أبوك. ثم قال (عليه السلام): عزّ و الله على عمك أن تدعوه فلا يجيبك أو يجيبك فلا ينفعك [أو يعينك فلا يغني عنك]. صوت و الله كثر واتره، و قلّ ناصره!

*Away with the people who have killed you! Who is their adversary on the Day of Judgement other than your grandfather and your father? By God, it saddens your uncle that you should call him while he cannot answer you, or that he answers but cannot help you, [or that he helps but cannot suffice you]. By God, our voice is one opposed by many and supported by few!*

ثم حمله و وضع صدره على صدره. و كأني أنظر إلى رجلي الغلام يخطان الأرض. فجاء به حتى ألقاه مع ابنه علي و القتلى من أهل بيته. ثم رفع طرفه إلى السماء و قال (عليه السلام):

[Al-Hussain (a)] carried [Al-Qasim], putting the boy's chest to his. It is as if I could see the boy's feet dragging on the floor. He carried him until he placed him with his son Ali [al-Akbar] and the rest of the fallen from his household. He raised his eyes to the heavens and said,

اللّهم أحصهم عددا و اقتلهم بددا و لا تغادر منهم أحدا [و لا تغفر لهم أبدا].

*My God, mark their numbers, kill them off bit by bit, do not leave any
of them [out of Your punishment, and do not ever forgive them].*

و صاح الحسين (عليه السلام) في تلك الحال:

In that condition, al-Hussain (a) called out,

صبرا يا بني عمومتي، صبرا يا أهل بيتي، فو الله لا رأيتم هوانا بعد هذا
اليوم أبدا.

*Be patient, my cousins! Be patient, O' members of my family! By God,
you will never experience meekness after this day.*[74]

# The Martyrdom of Some of Imam Hussain's (a) Brothers

و تقدمت إخوة الحسين (عليه السلام) عازمين على أن يموتوا دونه. فأول من خرج منهم أبو بكر بن علي (عليه السلام) و اسمه عبد الله، و أمه ليلى بنت مسعود من بني نهشل، فتقدم و هو يرتجز [...] فلم يزل يقاتل حتى قتله زجر بن بدر النخعي. ثم خرج من بعده أخوه عمر بن علي (عليه السلام)، أمه أم حبيب الصهباء بنت ربيعة التغلبية، فحمل على زجر قاتل أخيه فقتله، و استقبل القوم و جعل يضرب بسيفه ضربا منكرا، و هو [...] فلم يزل يقاتل حتى قتل.

Al-Hussain's (a) brothers stepped forward, intent on dying in his service and protection.

The first to rush into the battlefield was [Abdullah] ibn Ali (a), whose [nickname was Abu Bakr]. His mother was Layla bint Masood of the Nahshal clan. He rushed into the battlefield [declaring in verse his lineage and his intent to die in protection of his brother]. He continued to fight until he was killed by Zajr ibn Badr al-Nakha'ei.

Then his brother Omar ibn Ali (a) stepped forward. His mother was al-Sahba' bint Rabe'a al-Taghlibiyya [known as Umm Habib]. He charged toward Zajr, his brother's killer, and killed him. He rushed toward the enemies, swinging his sword with might and valor while [taunting his enemies with prideful verses]. He continued to fihgt until he was killed.

و خرج محمّد الأصغر بن علي (عليه السلام) و أمه أم ولد، فرماه رجل من تميم من بني أبان بن دارم، فقتله و جاء برأسه. و خرج عبد الله بن علي (عليه السلام) و أمه ليلى بنت مسعود النهشلية، فقاتل حتى قتل. و هو أخو أبي

بكر بن علي (ع) لأمه و أبيه، و هو غير عبد الله الأصغر بن علي (عليه السلام) شقيق العباس (عليه السلام)، كما صرح بذلك الشيخ المفيد في (الإرشاد).

Then Muhammad al-Asghar ibn Ali (a) [...] set out unto the battlefield. A man from the tribe of Tameem, from the descendants of Aban ibn Darim, struck him with an arrow and returned with his head.

Abdullah ibn Ali (a) stepped forward and fought until he was killed. His mother was Layla bint Masood al-Nahshaliyya and he was Abu Bakr ibn Ali's (a) full brother. He is not Abdullah al-Asghar ibn Ali (a), the full brother of al-Abbas, as was expressly stated by al-Shaykh al-Mufeed in *al-Irshaad*.[75]

# The Martyrdom of al-Abbas's Full Brothers

و لما رأى العباس بن علي (ع) كثرة القتلى من أهله قال لإخوته من أمه و أبيه،

و هم عبد الله و جعفر و عثمان (عليه السلام)، و أمهم أم البنين فاطمة بنت

حزام بن خالد الكلابية: يا بني أمي تقدموا حتى أراكم قد نصحتم لله و لرسوله،

فإنه لا ولد لكم [...]. فبرز عبد الله الأصغر بن علي (عليه السلام) و عمره

خمس و عشرون سنة و هو [يرتجز] فاختلف هو و هاني بن ثبيت الحضرمي

ضربتين، فقتله هاني.

When al-Abbas saw the great number of family members who had been martyred, he turned to his full brothers - Abdullah, Jafar, and Othman. Their mother was Fatima bint Hizam ibn Khalid al-Kilabiyya, known as Umm al-Baneen. He said to them, "O' sons of my mother, step forward so that I can see you be faithful to God and His Messenger (s); for you have no children [to worry about in case of your martyrdom]." [...]

Abdullah al-Asghar, a man of 25 years, stepped forward [while taunting the enemy with verses in praise of his father]. He fought Hani ibn Thubayt al-Hadrami, who slayed him.

ثم برز بعده أخوه جعفر بن علي (عليه السلام) و كان عمره تسع عشرة سنة

و هو [يرتجز] فحمل عليه هاني بن ثبيت الحضرمي أيضا فقتله، و جاء برأسه.

ثم برز بعده أخوه عثمان بن علي (عليه السلام) فقام مقام إخوته، و كان عمره

إحدى و عشرين سنة و هو [يرتجز] فرماه خولي بن يزيد الأصبحي على جبينه

فسقط عن فرسه، و حمل عليه رجل من بني أبان بن دارم فقتله، و جاء برأسه.

Then his brother Jafar ibn Ali (a), who was 19 years of age, stepped forward [reciting verses in praise of his family and declaring his intent to die protecting Imam Hussain (a)]. Hani ibn Thubayt al-Hadrami charged at him and killed him, returning with his head.

Their brother Othman ibn Ali (a), a man of 21, then stepped forward like his brothers [reciting verses in praise of his father, the Prophet (s), and Imam Hussain (a)]. Khawli ibn Yazid al-Asbahi shot him with an arrow to the forehead, knocking him off his horse. A man from the clan of Aban ibn Darim charged at him and killed him, returning with his head.[76]

# Al-Abbas Martyred While Seeking Water for the Camp

قال العباس (عليه السلام): قد ضاق صدري من هؤلاء المنافقين و أريد أن آخذ ثأري منهم. فأمره الحسين (عليه السلام) أن يطلب الماء للأطفال، فذهب العباس (عليه السلام) إلى القوم و وعظهم و حذّرهم غضب الجبار فلم ينفع، فنادى بصوت عال: يا عمر بن سعد هذا الحسين ابن بنت رسول الله، قد قتلتم أصحابه و أهل بيته، و هؤلاء عياله و أولاده عطاشى فاسقوهم من الماء، فقد أحرق الظمأ قلوبهم، و هو مع ذلك يقول:

Al-Abbas said, "I grow impatient with these hypocrites and I wish to seek redress against them." Al-Hussain (a) instructed him to fetch water for the children first. Al-Abbas went towards the enemy and advised them, warning them of the Almighty's wrath; but this was to no avail. He then called out, "O' Omar ibn Saad, this is al-Hussain (a), the son of the daughter of Messenger of God (s). You have killed his companions and family. His wards and children are thirsty, so give them some water to quench their burning hearts. All the while, [al-Hussain (a)] has been saying,

**دعوني أذهب إلى الروم أو الهند و أخلّي لكم الحجاز و العراق.**

*Let me go to Rome or India and leave Hijaz and Iraq to you."*

فأثّر كلام العباس (عليه السلام) في نفوس القوم حتى بكى بعضهم. و لكن الشمر صاح بأعلى صوته: يابن أبي تراب لو كان وجه الأرض كله ماء و هو تحت أيدينا لما سقيناكم منه قطرة، إلا أن تدخلوا في بيعة يزيد. ثم إنه ركب جواده و أخذ القربة، فأحاط به أربعة آلاف و رموه بالنبال.

Al-Abbas's words effected the hearts of the enemy such that some of them began to cry. Shimr, however, called out, "O' son of Abu Turab [Imam Ali (a)], if the face of the earth was all water and under our control, we would not give you a single drop unless you pledge allegiance to Yazid." [Al-Abbas] rode his horse and took the waterskin. He was surrounded by four thousand enemies who pelted him with arrows.

فلم ترعه كثرتهم و أخذ يطرد أولئك الجماهير وحده، و لواء الحمد يرفرف على رأسه، فلم تثبت له الرجال، و نزل إلى الفرات مطمئنا غير مبال بذلك الجمع. و لما اغترف من الماء ليشرب تذكّر عطش أخيه الحسين (عليه السلام) و من معه، فرمى الماء و قال:

Their numbers did not discourage him and he began to repel them by himself while the banner of glorification [to God Almighty] waved above his head. Men could not stand in his way and he was able to reach the Euphrates despite the great number amassed against him. But when he took a handful of water to drink, he remembered the thirst of his brother al-Hussain (a) and those with him. He threw the water back [into the river] and said,

يا نفس من بعد الحسين هوني * * * و بعده لا كنت أن تكوني

هذا الحسين وارد المنون * * * و تشربين بارد المعين

تالله ما هذا فعال ديني * * * و لا فعال صادق اليقين

*O' self, [be second] to al-Hussain (a)*

*As after him, it matters not whether you be or not*

*This is Hussain (a) approaching death*

*And you [dare] drink sweet, cold water?*

*By God, this is not an act of my faith*

*Nor an act of a man of true certainty*

ثم ملأ القربة و ركب جواده و توجّه نحو المخيم فقطع عليه الطريق، و جعل يضرب حتى أكثر القتل فيهم و كشفهم عن الطريق و هو يقول:

He filled the waterskin and rode his horse back towards the camp. Enemies blocked the way and he fended them off again, killing much of them. He would recite,

لا أرهب الموت إذا الموت رقى  * * *  حتى أوارى في المصاليت لقى

نفسي لسبط المصطفى الطهر وقى  * * *  إني أنا العباس أغدو بالسّقا

و لا أخاف الشرّ يوم الملتقى

*I do not fear death if it approached*

*Leaving brave men felled beside me*

*I will give my soul in protection of the Prophet's (s) pure grandson*

*I am al-Abbas, and I will return with the water*

*I do not fear harm on the day of battle*

فكمن له زيد بن الرقّاد الجهني من وراء نخلة و عاونه حكيم بن الطفيل السنبسي، فضربه على يمينه فبراها، فقال (عليه السلام):

Zaid ibn al-Raqqad al-Juhani and Hakeem ibn al-Tufail al-Sunbusi ambushed him from behind a palm tree. The struck him on his right arm, severing it. [But al-Abbas pushed on], saying,

و الله إن قطعتم يميني  * * *  إني أحامي أبدا عن ديني

و عن إمام صادق اليقين  * * *  سبط النبي الطاهر الأمين

*By God, if you have severed my right arm*

*I will continue to defend my faith*

*And [protecting] an Imam of true certainty*

*The grandson of the pure and trusted Prophet (s)*

فلم يعبأ بيمينه بعد أن كان همه إيصال الماء إلى أطفال الحسين (عليه السلام) و عياله، و لكن الحكيم بن الطفيل كمن له من وراء نخلة، فلما مرّ به ضربه على شماله فقطعها فقال (عليه السلام):

He did not give any attention to his severed right arm, as his sole concern was delivering the water to al-Hussain's (s) wards and children. But Hakeem ibn al-Tufail ambushed him once again from behind a palm tree, striking him on his left arm and severing it. [Yet al-Abbas continued to push on], saying,

يا نفس لا تخشي من الكفّار * * * و أبشري برحمة الجبّار

مع النبي السيد المختار * * * مع جملة السادات و الأطهار

قد قطّعوا بغيهم يساري * * * فأصلهم يا ربّ حرّ النار

*O' self, do not fear this band of disbelievers*

*And rejoice for the mercy of the Almighty*

*Alongside our master, the Chosen Prophet (s)*

*Along with the other noble and pure souls*

*They have severed my left arm by their wretchedness*

*O' Lord, deliver them to a blazing Hell!*

و تكاثروا عليه و أتته السهام كالمطر، فأصاب القربة سهم و أريق ماؤها، و سهم أصاب صدره و ضربه رجل بالعمود على رأسه ففلق هامته، و سقط على

الأرض ينادي: عليك مني السلام أبا عبد الله. فأتاه الحسين (عليه السلام) و
قد استشهد، فقال:

The enemies surrounded him as arrows rained down; one struck the
waterskin and spilling its water, while another struck him in his chest.
A man hit him on his head with a pole, cracking his skull. He fell to
the ground calling, "Farewell, O' Abu Abdullah (a)." Al-Hussain (a)
rushed to him and found that he had been martyred. He said,

الآن انكسر ظهري و قلّت حيلتي.

*Now my back has been broken and I have been left powerless.*[77]

# Imam Hussain (a) Bids Farewell to al-Abbas

أخذ الحسين (عليه السلام) رأسه و وضعه في حجره، و جعل يمسح الدم عن عينيه، فرآه و هو يبكي. فقال الحسين (عليه السلام):

Al-Hussain (a) took al-Abbas's head and placed it in his lap. He began to wipe the blood off his eyes and saw that he was crying. Al-Hussain (a) asked,

## ما يبكيك يا أبا الفضل؟

*What has made you cry, O' Abu al-Fadl?*

قال: يا نور عيني، و كيف لا أبكي و مثلك الآن جئتني و أخذت رأسي، فبعد ساعة من يرفع رأسك عن التراب، و من يمسح التراب عن وجهك! و كان الحسين (عليه السلام) جالسا، إذ شهق العباس شهقة، و فارقت روحه الطيبة. فصاح الحسين (عليه السلام):

[Al-Abbas] replied, "O' light of my eys! How can I not cry when you have come to me and taken my head [in your lap]? But in an hour who will lift you head from the ground and wipe the sand off your face?"Al-Hussain (a) was sitting there when al-Abbas took his last breath and his blessed soul departed his body. He cried out,

## وا أخاه، وا عباساه، وا ضيعتاه!

*O' my brother! O' Abbas! O' what a loss![78]*

# Historians Neglect the Account of al-Abbas's Martyrdom

أورد الخوارزمي في مقتله مصرع العباس باختصار كبير، ج 2 ص 29 قال: ثم
خرج من بعده العباس بن علي (عليه السلام) و أمه أم البنين، و هو السّقّاء،
لحمل و هو [يرتجز] فلم يزل يقاتل حتى قتل جماعة من القوم ثم قتل. فقال
الحسين (عليه السلام): الآن انكسر ظهري و قلّت حيلتي.

Al-Khawarizmi excerpted the account of al-Abbas's martyrdom in his *Maqtal* (v. 2 p. 29). He wrote "Then al-Abbas stepped forward, and his mother was Umm al-Baneen. He was in charge of maintaining the water supply. He charged, [declaring his intent to die protecting his brother in verse]. He continued to fight and killed a group of enemies but was killed. Al-Hussain (a) then said, 'Now my back has been broken and I have been left powerless.'"[79]

# The Martyrdom of the sons of al-Abbas ibn Ali (a)

ذكر السيد عبد الرزاق المقرم في كتابه (العباس قمر بني هاشم) ص 195: أنه
كان للعباس (عليه السلام) خمسة أولاد: الفضل و عبيد الله و الحسن و القاسم
و بنت واحدة. وعدّ ابن شهر اشوب في مناقبه من الشهداء يوم الطف من ولد
العباس (عليه السلام): محمّد بن العباس (عليه السلام) أمه لبابة بنت عبيد
الله بن العباس بن عبد المطلب. و ليس للعباس (عليه السلام) نسل إلا من
ولده عبيد الله.

Sayyid Abdulrazzaq al-Muqarram mentioned in his book *al-Abbas Qamar Bani Hashem* (p. 195), "Al-Abbas had five children; al-Fadl, Obaydillah, al-Hassan, al-Qasim, and a daughter."

Ibn Shahrashoob counted Muhammad ibn al-Abbas amongst the martyrs of Karbala in his book *al-Manaqib*. [Muhammad's mother was said to be] Lubaba bint Obaydillah ibn al-Abbas ibn Abdulmuttalib. Al-Abbas did not have any surviving lineage except through his son Obaydillah.[80]

# Al-Hussain's (a) Cry for Help

و لما قتل العباس (عليه السلام) التفت الحسين (عليه السلام) فلم ير أحدا
ينصره. و نظر إلى أهله و صحبه مجزّرين كالأضاحي، و هو إذ ذاك يسمع عويل
الأيامى و صراخ الأطفال، صاح بأعلى صوته:

After the martyrdom of al-Abbas, al-Hussain (a) looked around and
did not see anyone who would aid him. He saw his companions and
family members slaughtered like sacrificial lambs, while the wails of the
widows and the cries of the orphans rung in his ears. He cried in the
loudest of voices,

**هل من ذابّ يذبّ عن حرم رسول الله (صلى الله عليه و آله و**
**سلم)؟ هل من موحّد يخاف الله فينا؟ هل من مغيث يرجو الله في**
**إغاثتنا؟ هل من معين يرجو ما عند الله في إعانتنا؟**

*Is there a defender who will defend the sanctity of the family of the*
*Messenger of God (s)? Is there a monotheist who fears God [and will*
*stand with us]? Is there a helper who will seek God by helping us? Is*
*there an aid who will seek the rewards of God by aiding us?[81]*

# Al-Hussain (a) Bids the Hashemite Women Farewell

فدعا (عليه السلام) ببردة رسول الله (صلى الله عليه و آله و سلم) و التحف

بها، و أفرغ عليه درعه الفاضل، و تقلّد سيفه، و استوى على متن جواده و

هو غائص في الحديد. فأقبل على أم كلثوم (عليها السلام) و قال لها:

Al-Hussain (a) called for the mantle of the Messenger of God (s) and cloaked himself with it. He wore his blessed armor, carried his sword, and rode his horse, fully dressed in iron armor. He approached Umm Kulthum and said,

**أوصيك يا أخيّة بنفسك خيرا، و إني بارز إلى هؤلاء القوم.**

*Take care of yourself, sister. I am stepping forward to battle this group.*

فأقبلت سكينة و هي صارخة و كان يحبها حبا شديدا، فضمّها إلى صدره و

مسح دموعها بكمه، و قال:

[His daughter] Sukayna ran to him wailing, and he used to love her immensly. He hugged her, wiped her tears with his sleave, and said [in verse],

سيطول بعدي يا سكينة فاعلمي * * * منك البكاء إذا الحمام دهاني

لا تحرقي قلبي بدمعك حسرة * * * ما دام مني الروح في جثماني

فإذا قتلت فأنت أولى بالذي * * * تأتينه يا خيرة النسوان

*Know, O' Sukayna, that after me you will*

*Cry much, when death will over come me*

*Do not burn my heart with your agonizing tears*

*So long as my soul remains in my body*

*If I were slain, you will more justly*

*Continue your cries, O' best of women*[82]

# Al-Hussain (a) Elegizes Himself

ثم نادى (عليه السلام):

Al-Hussain (a) then cried out,

**يا أم كلثوم و يا زينب و يا سكينة و يا رقية و يا عاتكة و يا صفية، عليكنّ مني السلام، فهذا آخر الاجتماع، و قد قرب منكن الافتجاع.**

*O' Umm Kulthum. O' Zaynab. O' Sukayna. O' Ruqaya. O' 'Atika. O' Safiyya. I bid you farewell, for this is our last meeting. You will soon be grieving.*

فصاحت أم كلثوم: يا أخي كأنك استسلمت للموت! فقال لها الحسين (عليه السلام):

Umm Kulthum cried out, "Brother! It is as if you have submitted to death!" Al-Hussain (a) said to her,

**يا أختاه فكيف لا يستسلم من لا ناصر له و لا معين!**

*How can one who does not have a helper nor an aid not submit to death?*

فقالت: يا أخي ردّنا إلى حرم جدنا. فقال لها:

She said, "Then return us to the [city] of our grandfather." He replied,

**يا أختاه هيهات هيهات، لو ترك القطا ليلا لنام.**

*O' Sister! Woe! Woe! [If there was any possible way for me to fulfill your wish, I surely would have].*

رفعت سكينة صوتها بالبكاء و النحيب، فضمّها الحسين (عليه السلام) إلى صدره الشريف و قبّلها و مسح دموعها بكمّه.

Sukayna began to cry and wail. Al-Hussain (a) hugged her, kissed her, and wiped her tears with his sleeve.[83]

فلما سمعته زينب (عليها السلام) بكت، و جرى الدموع من عينيه، و نادت: وا وحدتاه، وا قلة ناصراه، وا سوء منقلباه، وا شؤم صباحاه. فشقّت ثوبها و نشرت شعرها و لطمت على وجهها. فقال الحسين (عليه السلام):

When [Lady] Zaynab heard him, she cried. Tears flowed in his eyes. She cried out, "O' solitude! O' lack of support! O' dreadful end! O' cursed morn!" She tore her dress, disheveled her hair, and struck her face.* Al-Hussain (a) said to her,

مهلا لها، يا بنت المرتضى، إن البكاء طويل.

*Have patience, O' daughter of al-Murtada. There is much time for weeping.*

فأراد أن يخرج من الخيمة، فلصقت به زينب (عليها السلام) فقالت: مهلا يا أخي، توقّف حتى أزوّد حتى من نظري، و أودّعك وداع مفارق لا تلاق بعده... فمهلا يا أخي قبل الممات هنيهة، لتبرد مني لوعة و غليل. فجعلت تقبّل يديه و رجليه. و أحطن به سائر النسوان...

He wanted to walk out of the tent, but she rushed to him and said, "Wait, brother! Stay so my sight can take its fill of you and so I can bid you the proper farewell after which we will never meet again... Wait here brother before rushing to death so that I can cool my anguish and thirst." She began to kiss his hands and feet as he was surrounded by the rest of the women.[84]

---

* Lady Zaynab was still in her tent when this took place.

# Al-Hussain (a) Wears a Worn Cloth under his Clothes

ثم قال (عليه السلام) لأخته:

Al-Hussain (a) then said to his sister,

اتيني بثوب عتيق لا يرغب فيه أحد من القوم، أجعله تحت ثيابي لئلا أجرّد منه بعد قتلي.

*Bring me an old piece of cloth that no one would want and that I can
wear under my clothes so that I would not be robbed of it after my death.*

فارتفعت أصوات النساء بالبكاء و النحيب. فأتوه بتبّان، فلم يرغب فيه لأنه من
لباس الذلة. و أخذ ثوبا خلقا [أي باليا] و خرّقه و جعله تحت ثيابه، و دعا
بسراويل حبرة ففزرها و لبسها لئلا يسلب منها.

The voices of the women rose in cries and wails. They brought him a
short trouser, but he refused it as it was a mark of humiliation. He took
a piece of worn out clothing, ripped it, and wore it under his clothes.
He called for knitted trousers and tore them before wearing them so
that he would not be robbed of them.

# Zayn al-Abideen (a) Attempts to Enter Battle Despite Illness

ثم التفت الحسين (عليه السلام) عن يمينه و شماله فلم ير أحدا من الرجال.

فخرج علي ابن الحسين (عليها السلام) و هو زين العابدين- و هو أصغر من

أخيه علي القتيل- و كان مريضا بالذّرب. و نهض السجّاد (عليه السلام) يتوكّأ

على عصا و يجّر سيفه، لأنه لا يقدر على حمله لمرضه، و أم كلثوم تنادي خلفه:

يا بني ارجع. فقال:

Al-Hussain (a) looked left and right, but could not see a single man by his side. Ali ibn al-Hussain (a) - known as Zayn al-Abideen (a) and the younger brother of Ali al-Akbar - who was stricken by a stomach illness came out of his tent. He was leaning on a walking stick and dragging his sword, as he could not carry it due to his illness. Umm Kulthm was running behind him calling, "Come back, my son!" He replied,

يا عمتاه! ذريني أقاتل بين يدي ابن بنت رسول الله (صلى الله عليه و آله و سلم).

*O' aunt. Leave me fight before the son of the daughter of the Messenger of God (s).*

فصاح الحسين (عليه السلام) بأم كلثوم:

Al-Hussain (a) called to Umm Kulthum,

احبسيه لئلا تخلو الأرض من نسل آل محمّد (صلى الله عليه و آله و سلم).

*Restrain him so that the earth is not deprived of the lineage of the family of Muhammad (s).*

فأرجعته إلى فراشه.

Umm Kulthum took him back to his bed.[85]

# The Martyrdom of the Infant Abdullah

ثم تقدم (عليه السلام) إلى باب الخيمة و قال:

Al-Hussain (a) then went to the tent and said,

### ناولوني ولدي الرضيع لأودعه.

*Hand me my infant son so that I can bid him farewell.*

فأتته زينب (عليها السلام) بابنه عبد الله [و قد سمّاه ابن شهر اشوب: علي الأصغر] و أمه الرباب بنت امرئ القيس، فأجلسه في حجره و جعل يقبّله و يقول:

[Lady] Zaynab came to him with his son Abdullah [who was called by Ibn Shahrashoob 'Ali al-Asghar'], whose mother was al-Rabab bint Imra' al-Qays. He took him in his arms and kissed him, saying,

### بعدا لهؤلاء القوم، إذا كان خصمهم جدك المصطفى.

*May God distance these people [from His mercy], as their adversary [on the Day of Judgment will be] your great-grandfather al-Mustafa (s).*

ثم أتى (عليه السلام) بالرضيع نحو القوم يطلب له الماء، و قال لهم:

He took the infant and approach the enemy, asking them to give him some water. He said to them,

### لقد جفّت محالب أمه، فهل إلى شربة من ماء سبيل؟ [...] يا قوم، إذا كنت أقاتلكم و تقاتلونني، فما ذنب هذا الطفل حتى تمنعوا عنه الماء؟!

*His mother's milk has dried up, so is there a way for him to have a sip of water? [...] O' people, if I fight you and you fight me, what is the crime of this child that you deny him water?*

(و في رواية) أنه قال:

Another narrations states that he said,

## إذا لم ترحموني فارحموا هذا الطفل.

*If you will not have mercy on me, then have mercy on this child.*

فمنهم من رقّ قلبه للطفل، و قال: اسقوه شربة من ماء، و منهم من قال: لا تسقوه و لا ترحموه! فخاف عمر بن سعد أن يدبّ النزاع في صفوف جيشه، فقال لحرملة بن كاهل الأسدي و كان راميا: اقطع نزاع القوم.

Some amongst them felt sympathetic and said, "Give him a sip of water." Other said, "Do not give him water or show him ant mercy!" Omar ibn Saad feared that there would be discord in the ranks of his army. He turned to Harmala ibn Kahil al-Asadi, a well-known archer, and said, "End these people's dispute!"

فسدد حرملة سهمه نحو عنق الصبي، فرماه بسهم فذبحه من الوريد إلى الوريد، و هو لائذ بحجر أبيه. فأخذ الطفل يفحص من ألم الجروح، و يرفرف كما يرفرف الطير المذبوح، و دمه يشخب من أوداجه، و الحسين (عليه السلام) يتلقّى دمه من نحره حتى امتلأت كفه، ثم رمى به نحو السماء. قال الإمام الباقر (عليه السلام):

Harmala aimed his arrow at the boy's neck. The arrow stuck the infant and severed his jugular as he was in his father's arms. The infant began to squirm with pain, fluttering like a wounded bird. Blood flowed from his veins and al-Hussain (a) took it in his hands. He threw a handful of blood to the sky. Imam al-Baqir (a) said,

فما وقع منه قطرة إلى الأرض، و لو وقعت منه إلى الأرض قطرة لنزل العذاب.

*Not a drop of [that blood] fell to earth. If a single drop had touched the earth, [God's] punishment would have befell [the enemy army].*

ثم قال (عليه السلام):

[Al-Hussain (a)] then said,

هوّن ما نزل بي أنه بعين الله تعالى. اللّهم لا يكن أهون عليك من فصيل ناقة صالح. إلهي إن كنت حبست عنا النصر [من السماء]، فاجعله لما هو خير منه، و انتقم لنا من [هؤلاء القوم] الظالمين و اجعل ما حلّ بنا في العاجل ذخيرة لنا في الآجل. اللّهم أنت الشاهد على قوم قتلوا أشبه الناس برسولك محمّد (صلى الله عليه و آله و سلم).

*What has befallen me is only eased because it is all in the eyes of God. O' God, [let this infant] not be of less significance to you than the calf of Saleh's she-camel. O' God, if you have kept victory away from us, then let it be for something greater. Exact our vengeance from the oppressors. Let what has befallen us in the present be our provision for the Hereafter. O' God, be witness to a people who have killed the one most similar to Your Messenger Muhammad (s).*

فسمع (عليه السلام) مناديا من السماء:

He heard a caller from the heavens say,

دعه يا حسين فإن له مرضعا في الجنة.

*Leave him, O' Hussain (a), for he has a wet-nurse [awaiting him] in paradise!*

ثم نزل (عليه السلام) عن فرسه، و حفر له بجفن سيفه، و دفنه مرمّلا بدمه،

و صلّى عليه. و يقال: وضعه مع قتلى أهل بيته.

[Al-Hussain (a)] came down from his horse, dug a grave with the sheath of his sword, buried the child covered in dust and blood, and prayed over him. It is also said that he put him with the rest of the martyrs of his family.[86]

# Al-Hussain (a) Mourns his Martyred Companions

ثم توجّه (عليه السلام) نحو القوم و قال:

[Al-Hussain (a)] then turned to the enemy and said,

يا ويلكم علام تقاتلوني؛ على حقّ تركته، أم على سنّة غيّرتها، أم على
شريعة بدّلتها؟!

*Woe to you! Why do you fight me? For a truth that I have abondened?
Or for a tradition that I have replaced? Or for a divine ruling that I
have changed?*

فقالوا: بل نقاتلك بغضا منا لأبيك و ما فعل بأشياخنا يوم بدر و حنين. فلما
سمع كلامهم بكى و جعل ينظر يمينا و شمالا فلم ير أحدا من أنصاره إلا من صافح
التراب جبينه، و من قطع الحمام أنينه. فنادى:

They replied, "We fight you out of hatred for your father and for what
he did to our elders on the days of Badr and Hunayn." When he heard
their words, he began to cry and looked left and right. He did not find
any of his companions that had not embraced the dust and had death
end his sighs. He cried out,

يا مسلم بن عقيل و يا هانئ بن عروة و يا حبيب بن مظاهر و يا
زهير بن القين [...]يا أبطال الصفا، و يا فرسان الهيجا، مالي أناديكم
فلا تجيبون، و أدعوكم فلا تسمعون! أنتم نيام، أرجوكم تنتبهون، أم
حالت مودتكم عن إمامكم فلا تنصروه! هذه نساء الرسول (صلى الله
عليه و آله و سلم) لفقدكم قد علاهن النحول.

O' Muslim ibn Aqeel! O' Hani ibn Urwa! O' Habib ibn Mudhahir!
O' Zuhair ibn al-Qayn! [...] O' heroes in times of peace! O' knights in
times of war! Why is it that I call you and you do not answer? Why do
I cry out to you and you do not listen? If you are asleep, please awaken!
Has your love for your Imam been shaken so that you are not aiding
him? These are the women of the [family of the] Messenger of God (s),
weakened by your absence.

فقوموا عن نومتكم أيها الكرام، و ادفعوا عن حرم الرسول الطغاة اللئام.
و لكن صرعكم و الله ريب المنون، و غدر بكم الدهر الخؤون، و إلا
لما كنتم عن نصرتي تقصّرون، و لا عن دعوتي تحتجبون. فها نحن
عليكم مفتجعون، و بكم لاحقون. فإنا لله و إنا إليه راجعون.

Wake up from your slumber, O' most honorable of men! Repel these evil
tyrants away from the family of the Messenger of God (s)! Alas! By
God, the calamities of the time have beaten you! This treacherous age
has betrayed you! Otherwise, you would not fall short in aiding me! You
would not ignore my calls! We are bereaved [at your loss] and will soon
follow you. Indeed, we are of God and to Him we shall return.[87]

# The Martyrdom of al-Hussain

# Verses of Poetry from al-Hussain (a)

ثم وثب (عليه السلام) قائمًا، و [إمتدح جده رسول الله (ص) وأباه أمير المؤمنين (ع) وأمه فاطمة الزهراء]. ثم حمل (عليه السلام) على الميمنة، و هو يقول:

Al-Hussain (a) then stood and [recited verses of poetry in praise of his grandfather the Prophet (s), his father the Commander of the Faihtful (a), and his mother Lady Fatima (a)]. He then charged at the enemy's right flank, saying,

الموت أولى من ركوب العار * * * و العار أولى من دخول النار

و الله من هذا و هذا جاري

*Death is better than living in humiliation*

*And humiliation is better than entering hellfire*

*But God is my refuge from both these ills!*

و حمل على الميسرة، و هو يقول:

He charged at the enemy's left flank, saying,

أنا الحسين بن علي * * * آليت ألا أنثني

أحمي عيالات أبي * * * أمضي على دين النبي

*I am al-Hussain ibn Ali (a)!*

*I have sworn not to bend [to my enemies]!*

*I will protect the family of my father!*

*I will continue on the religion of the Prophet (s).[88]*

# An Arrow Strikes al-Hussain's (a) Jaw (1)

و اشتدّ العطش بالحسين فمنعوه. فحصل له شربة ماء، فلما أهوى ليشرب رماه
حصين بن نمير بسهم في حنكه، فصار الماء دما. ثم رفع يده إلى السماء و هو
يقول:

Thirst overpowered al-Hussain (a), but the enemies blocked him [from reaching the river]. He was finally able to acquire a bit of water, but when he attempted to drink it Hossayn ibn Numair struck him with an arrow in his jaw. Blood flowed into the water [and he was no longer able to drink it]. Al-Hussain (a) then raised his hands to the heavens and said,

اللّهم أحصهم عددا، و اقتلهم بددا، و لا تذر على الأرض منهم أحدا.

*O' God, tally their number, kill them in small groups, and do not leave a single one of them on this earth!*[89]

# An Arrow Strikes al-Hussain's (a) Jaw (2)

و اشتد العطش بالحسين (عليه السلام) فركب المسناة يريد الفرات، فاعترضته

خيل ابن سعد، فرمى رجل من بني دارم الحسين (عليه السلام) بسهم، فأثبته

في حنكه الشريف، فانتزع السهم و بسط يديه تحت حنكه حتى امتلأت راحتاه

من الدم، ثم رمى به و قال:

Thirst overpowered al-Hussain (a) so he rode towards the river bank. The cavalry of Ibn Saad cut off his route and a man from Banu Darim shot him with an arrow that struck his noble jaw. He pulled out the arrow and placed his hands under his jaw until his palms were filled with blood. He then threw it toward the heavens and said,

اللّهم إني أشكو إليك ما يفعل بابن بنت نبيك.

*O' God, I complain to you of what is being done to the son of You Prophet's (s) daughter!*[90]

# Al-Hussain (a) was Killed Thirsty

و منعوا الحسين (عليه السلام) من الماء في يوم شديد الحر، و صاروا يتراءون
إليه بكيزان من البلور مملوءة ماء باردا، فيقول:

[The enemy army] cut off water from al-Hussain (a) on a day of severe heat. They began to parade crystalline cups filled with cold water as he would say,

أقسم عليكم بجدّي إلا سقيتموني شربة أبرّد بها كبدي.

*I swear to you by my grandfather that you should give me a sip to cool my body!*

فلم يجيبوه.

They would not answer his call.[91]

# Thirst Takes its Toll on al-Hussain (a)

و لقد أثّر العطش في الحسين (عليه السلام) في أربعة مواضع من أعضائه
الشريفة: الكبد و الشقّة و اللسان و العين. الشفة ذابلة من الأوام، و الكبد
مفتّت من حرّ الظمأ، و اللسان مجروح من كثرة اللوك في الفم، و العين من
شدة العطش مظلمة.

Thirst affected al-Hussain (a) in four areas of his noble body; his livers,
lips, tongue, and eyes. His lips were withered and his liver was severly
damaged due to thirst. His tongue was gashed [due to the failure of his
salvitory glands]. His eyesight was blurred [due to dehydration].[92]

# Al-Hussain (a) is Cut Off from his Camp

ثم إنه (عليه السلام) دعا الناس إلى البراز، فلم يزل يقتل كلّ من دنا إليه من عيون الرجال، حتى قتل منهم مقتلة عظيمة، فحالوا بينه و بين رحله، فصاح بهم:

Al-Hussain (a) then called the enemy to duel. He continued to fell any warrior who would approach him until he killed a great many of them. The enemy then cut him off from his camp. Al-Hussain (a) called out,

**و يحكم يا شيعة آل أبي سفيان، إن لم يكن لكم دين، و كنتم لا تخافون المعاد، فكونوا أحرارا في دنياكم هذه، و ارجعوا إلى أحسابكم إن كنتم عربا كما تزعمون!**

*Woe to you, followers of Abu Sufyan's family! If you have no religion and you do not fear the Resurrection, then [at least] be free in this world of yours! Return to your roots if you are Arabs as you claim!*

فناداه شمر: ما تقول يا حسين؟ فقال (عليه السلام):

Al-Shimr asked, "What are you saying, O' Hussain (a)?" He replied,

**أقول أنا الّذي أقاتلكم و تقاتلوني، و النساء ليس عليهن جناح، فامنعوا عتاتكم و طغاتكم و جهّالكم عن التعرّض لحرمي ما دمت حيّا.**

*I say that I am the one fighting you and you are fighting me. The women have committed no crime. Forbid your defiant, savage, and ignorant [soldiers] from attacking my family so long as I live!*

قال له شمر: لك ذلك يابن فاطمة. ثم صاح شمر بأصحابه: إليكم عن حرم الرجل و اقصدوه بنفسه، فلعمري لهو كفو كريم.

Al-Shimr said, "You shall have that, O' son of Fatima (a)." Then he looked at his soldiers and cried out, "Leave the man's family and attack him! By my life, he is a noble opponent!"[93]

# The Enemies Deceive al-Hussain (a)

فقصده القوم، و هو مع ذلك يطلب شربة من الماء. و كلما حمل بفرسه على
الفرات حملوا عليه بأجمعهم فلّؤوه عنه. ثم حمل على الأعور السلمي و عمرو بن
الحجاج و كانا في أربعة آلاف رجل، على الشريعة ففرّقهم، و ألقم الفرس في
الفرات. فلما ولغ الفرس برأسه ليشرب، قال (عليه السلام):

The enemies charged at him while he continued to seek a drink of
water. Whenever he approached the Euphrates on his horse, the
enemy would charge at him and repel him [from the river].

Al-Hussain (a) then charged at al-A'war al-Salami and Amr ibn al-
Hajjaj, who were commanding four thousand men. He scrambled their
troops and rode his horse into the Euphrates. When the horse lowered
its head to drink, al-Hussain (a) said,

أنت عطشان و أنا عطشان، و الله لا ذقت حتى تشرب!

*You are thirsty and I am thirsty. By God, I will not drink until you do!*

فرفع الفرس رأسه كأنه فهم الكلام. فقال الحسين (عليه السلام):

The horse raised its head as if it had understood his words. Al-Hussain
(a) then said,

اشرب.

*Drink!*

و لما مدّ الحسين (عليه السلام) يده فغرف من الماء غرفة ليشرب، ناداه رجل
من القوم: يا أبا عبد الله، أتتلذّذ بشرب الماء و قد هتك حرمك؟! فنفض الماء
من يده، و حمل على القوم فكشفهم، فإذا الخيمة سالمة، فعلم أنها حيلة.

And when al-Hussain (a) took a handful of water to drink, an enemy soldier called out, "O' Abu Abdullah (a)! Do you saver a drink of water while your family is being attacked?" He threw the water in his hand and charged at the enemy, repelling them [from his way]. [When he got to the camp] he saw that the tents were safe and knew that the enemy had deceived him.[94]

# A Second Farewell

ثم إنه (عليه السلام) ودّع عياله ثانياً، و أمرهم بالصبر و لبس الأزر، و قال:

Al-Hussain (a) then bade farewell to his family again, instructing them to remain patient and perseverant. He said,

استعدوا للبلاء، و اعلموا أن الله تعالى حاميكم و حافظكم و سينجيكم من شرّ الأعداء، و يجعل عاقبة أمركم إلى خير، و يعذّب عدوكم بأنواع العذاب، و يعوّضكم عن هذه البلية بأنواع النعم و الكرامة، فلا تشكوا، و لا تقولوا بألسنتكم ما ينقص من قدركم.

*Be ready for tribulation. Know that God Almighty will guard and protect you, saving you from the evils of the enemy. He will deliver you to a great end. He will punish your enemy with all kinds of punishments. He will reward you for this trial with all kinds of blessings and honors. So do not complain and do not say with your own tongues what would reduce of your status.*

فقال ابن سعد: و يحكم اهجموا عليه مادام مشغولاً بنفسه و حرمه، و الله إن فرغ لكم لا تمتاز ميمنتكم عن ميسرتكم. فحملوا عليه يرمونه بالسهام، حتى تخالفت السهام بين أطناب الخيم. و شكّ سهم بعض أزر [جمع إزار] النساء، فدهشن و أرعبن و صحن، و دخلن الخيمة ينظرن إلى الحسين (عليه السلام) كيف يصنع.

Omar ibn Saad then said [to his soldiers], "Woe to you! Attack him while he is preoccupied with himself and his family. By God, if he were to turn to you, [he would scatter you so that] your right flank will be indistinguishable from your left!"

They attacked him, pelting him with arrows that ripped through the tents. Some tents ripped through the veils of the women. They began to cry, startled and terrified. They rushed to al-Hussain's (a) tent to see what he will do.[95]

# An Arrow Strikes al-Hussain's (a) Forehead

فقصده القوم بالحرب من كل جانب، فجعل يحمل عليهم و يحملون عليه، و هو

في ذلك يطلب الماء ليشرب منه شربة، فكلما حمل بفرسه على الفرات حملوا

عليه حتى أجلوه عنه. ثم رماه رجل يقال له أبو الحتوف الجعفي بسهم فوقع السهم

في جبهته (و في مقتل أبي مخنف: أن الّذي رماه هو خولي، و قيل إنه قدامة

العامري). فنزع الحسين (عليه السلام) السهم و رمى به، فسال الدم على وجهه

و لحيته. فقال:

The enemies attacked al-Hussain (a) from every direction. He charged
at them as they charged at him. He would try to charge toward the river
to get a drink, but whenever his horse approached the Euphrates, the
enemies would charge at him and repel him from the river.

Then a man name Abu al-Hutuf al-Ju'fi shot him with an arrow that
hit him in the forehead [Abu Makhnaf says the archer was Khawli,
while others say it was Qudama al-Amiri]. Al-Hussain (a) pulled the
arrow out and threw it to the ground, while blood gushed on his face
and beard. He said,

اللّهم قد ترى ما أنا فيه من عبادك هؤلاء العصاة العتاة، اللّهم فأحصهم
عددا، و اقتلهم بددا، و لا تذر على وجه الأرض منهم أحدا، و لا تغفر
لهم أبدا.

*O' God, You see what I suffer at the hands of your disobedient and
defiant servants! O' God, tally their number, kill them in small groups,
do not leave a single one of them on this earth, and do not ever forgive
their misdeeds!*

ثم حمل عليهم كالليث المغضب، فجعل لا يلحق أحدا إلا بعجه بسيفه و ألحقه
بالحضيض، و السهام تأخذه من كل ناحية، و هو يتلقاها بنحره و صدره و
يقول:

He charged at the enemy like an angered lion. He would strike each
man once with his sword and fell him. All the while, arrows rained
down on him from every direction, striking him in his chest and neck.
He would say,

يا أمة السوء، بئسما خلّفتم محمدا في عترته. أما إنكم لن تقتلوا بعدي
عبدا من عباد الله الصالحين فتهابوا قتله، بل يهون عليكم عند قتلكم
إياي. و ايم الله إني لأرجو أن يكرمني ربي بهوانكم، ثم ينتقم منكم من
حيث لا تشعرون.

*O' nation of misfortune! How wrongly you have treated Muhammad's*
*(s) family after his passing! Surely, you will never kill any of God's*
*righteous servants after me and fear the consequence. Rather, it will pale*
*in comparison after you kill me. By God, I hope that my Lord will honor*
*me through your demise, and that He should avenge me while you are*
*unaware [of His reprisal]!*

فصاح به الحصين بن مالك السكوني: يابن فاطمة، بماذا ينتقم لك منا؟ فقال
(عليه السلام):

Al-Hossayn ibn Malik al-Sakuni asked him, "O' son of Fatima (a)! How
will He avenge you?" He said,

يلقي بأسكم بينكم، و يسفك دماءكم، ثم يصبّ عليكم العذاب الأليم.

*He will turn your enmity toward one another, [so that you] shed [each*
*other's] blood. He will then heap upon you a most painful punishment.*

(و في مقتل المقرم، ص 350) قال: و رجع إلى مركزه يكثر من قول:

Al-Muqarram says in his *Maqtal* (p. 350): Then he returned to his base, continuously saying,

لا حول و لا قوة إلا بالله العلي العظيم.

*There is no power or authority save from God, the Most High and Glorious.*

و طلب في هذا الحال ماء، فقال الشمر: لا تذوقه حتى ترد النار. و ناداه رجل:
يا حسين ألا ترى الفرات كأنه بطون الحيات؟ فلا تشرب منه حتى تموت
عطشا! فقال الحسين (عليه السلام):

In this state, he asked [the enemy] for water, but al-Shimr said, "You will not taste it until you reach hellfire!" Another man called out, "O' Hussain, do you not see the Euphrates [flowing] like the belly of a snake? You will not drink of it until you die of thirst!" Al-Hussain (a) said,

اللهم أمته عطشا.

*O' God, kill him of thirst.*

فكان ذلك الرجل يطلب الماء، فيؤتى به فيشرب حتى يخرج من فيه، و ما زال
كذلك إلى أن مات عطشا.

[Afterwards], that man would continue to ask for water and drink until it would spew out of his mouth. He was like this until he died thirsty.[96]

# The Enemies Split into Three Divisions

إن الشمر أقبل إلى ابن سعد و قال له: أيها الأمير إن هذا الرجل يفنينا عن
آخرنا مبارزة. قال: كيف نصنع به؟. قال: نتفرّق عليه ثلاث فرق: فرقة بالنبال
و السهام، و فرقة بالسيوف و الرماح، و فرقة بالنار و الحجارة، نعجل عليه.
فجعلوا يرشقونه بالسهام، و يطعنونه بالرماح، و يضربونه بالسيوف، حتى أثخنوه
بالجراح.

Al-Shimr approached Ibn Saad and said, "Commander, this man will
kill us all [if we continue to] duel him [one by one]." Ibn Saad asked,
"So what should we do?" Al-Shimr replied, "We should split against
him into three divisions; one [to pelt him] with arrows and bolts, one
[to strike him] with swords and spears, and one [to attack him] with
fire and stones. Thus, we will soon fell him." They began to pelt him
with their arrows, stab him with their spears, and strike him with their
swords until he was overcome with wounds.[97]

# Al-Hussain's (a) Bravery and Resolve

فشدّ عليه رجّالة ممن عن يمينه و شماله، فحمل على من عن يمينه حتى ابذعرّوا،
و على من عن شماله حتى ابذعرّوا، و عليه قميص له من خز، و هو معتمّ.

Infantrymen charged at him from left and right. He charged at his enemies at the right and fought them until he repelled them. He charged at his enemies at the left and fought them until he repelled them. He was wearing a woolen robe and a turban.[98]

# Al-Hussain (a) on the Battlefield

قال عبد الله بن عمار بن يغوث: [فو الله] ما رأيت مكثورا قط، قد قتل ولده و أهل بيته و صحبه، أربط جأشا منه، و لا أمضى جنانا، و لا أجرأ مقدما. و لقد كانت الرجال تنكشف بين يديه إذا شدّ فيها، و لم يثبت له أحد.

Abdullah ibn Ammar ibn Yaghuth said, "By God, I have not seen a man outnumbered so, with his sons, kin, and companions all murdered, with stronger resolve, nor a more firm heart, nor more valor in his actions! Men would scatter before him if he charge at them so that no man stood before him!"

و إن كانت الرجال لتشدّ عليه فيشدّ عليها بسيفه، فتنكشف عنه انكشاف المعزى إذا شدّ فيها الذئب. و لقد كان يحمل فيهم و قد تكمّلوا ثلاثين ألفا، فينهزمون بين يديه كأنهم الجراد المنتشر، ثم يرجع إلى مركزه و هو يقول:

Men would charge at him and he would charge at them, scattering them like sheep attacked by a wolf. He would charge at an army of thirty thousand men and scatter them like a swarm of locust. He would then return to his base, saying,

## لا حول و لا قوة إلا بالله.

*There is no power or authority save in God, the Most High and Glorious!*

و لم يزل يقاتل حتى قتل ألف رجل و تسعمائة و خمسين رجلا، سوى المجروحين. فقال عمر بن سعد لقومه: الويل لكم، أتدرون لمن تقاتلون؟ هذا ابن الأنزع البطين، هذا ابن قتّال العرب، احملوا عليه (حملة رجل واحد) من كل جانب. فأتته أربعة آلاف نبلة.

He continued to fight until he killed one thousand, nine hundred, and fifty men and wounded others.

Omar ibn Saad then said, "Woe to you, do you know who you are fighting? This is the son of [Ali ibn Abu Talib (a)]! This is the son of the killer of Arabs! Charge at him at once from every direction." [Omar Ibn Saad's army shot at al-Hussain (a)] with four thousand arrows.[99]

# A Poisoned Arrow Strikes al-Hussain (a)

ثم جعل (عليه السلام) يقاتل حتى أصابته اثنتان و سبعون جراحة، فوقف يستريح و قد ضعف عن القتال. فبينا هو واقف إذ أتاه حجر فوقع على جبهته، فسالت الدماء من جبهته. فأخذ الثوب ليمسح [الدم] عن جبهته، فأتاه سهم محدّد مسموم له ثلاث شعب، فوقع في قلبه [و قيل في صدره]. فقال الحسين (عليه السلام):

Al-Hussain (a) continued to fight until he had been wounded seventy two times. He became too weak to fight and stopped to rest. As he was resting, a stone struck him on the forehead and blood began to rush out of the wound. As he took a piece of his clothes to wipe his forehead, a sharp, poisoned, three pronged arrow struck him in the chest. Al-Hussain (a) said,

بسم الله و بالله و على ملّة رسول الله.

*In the name of God! [I rely] on God and follow the religion of the Messenger of God (s)!*

و رفع رأسه إلى السماء، و قال:

He then raised his head to the heavens and said,

إلهي إنك تعلم أنهم يقتلون رجلا ليس على وجه الأرض ابن نبي غيره.

*O' God, You surely know that they are killing a man while knowing that there is no son of a prophet on the face of the earth but him!*

ثم أخذ السهم و أخرجه من وراء ظهره، فانبعث الدم كالميزاب، فوضع يده على الجرح، فلما امتلأت دما رمى به إلى السماء، فما رجع من ذلك قطرة. و ما عرفت

الحمرة في السماء حتى رمى الحسين (عليه السلام) بدمه إلى السماء. ثم وضع يده
على الجرح ثانيا، فلما امتلأت لطّخ بها رأسه و لحيته، و قال:

He took the arrow and drew it out from his back while his blood
flowed like a fountain. He put his hand on the wound until it was filled
with blood, then threw the blood toward the heavens. Not a drop of
it fell back to the earth. Redness was not seen in the sky before al-
Hussain (a) threw his blood toward it. He then placed his hand on the
wound again. When his hand was filled with blood, he took it and
stained his head and beard with it, saying,

هكذا و الله أكون حتى ألقى جدي محمدا و أنا مخضوب بدمي، و أقول:
يا رسول الله قتلني فلان و فلان.

*By God, this is how I will meet my grandfather Muhammad (s), stained
in my own blood! I will say, 'O' Messenger of God (s), I was killed by
so and so."*[100]

# Al-Hussain (a) is Struck on the Head

ثم ضعف (عليه السلام) عن القتال فوقف مكانه، فكلما أتاه رجل من الناس و

انتهى إليه، انصرف عنه و كره أن يلقى الله بدمه. حتى جاءه رجل من كندة

يقال له (مالك بن نسر) فضربه بالسيف على رأسه، و كان عليه برنس [أي

قلنسوة طويلة] فقطع البرنس و امتلأ دما، فقال له الحسين (عليه السلام):

Al-Hussain (a) became too weak to fight, so he stopped to rest. Enemy soldiers would come to him [to kill him], but they would soon retreat hating to meet God with his blood [on their hands]. Soon a man from Kinda named Malik ibn Nisr came to al-Hussain (a) and struck him on his head, tearing his headpiece in two and filling it with blood. Al-Hussain (a) said to him,

**لا أكلت بيمينك و لا شربت بها، و حشرك الله مع الظالمين.**

*May you never eat or drink with your right hand! May God group you along with the oppressors [on Judgment Day]!*

ثم ألقى البرنس و لبس قلنسوة و اعتمّ عليها، و قد أعيى و تبلّد... (و في بعض

الأخبار): أنه ألقى البرنس من رأسه، ثم جاء إلى الخيمة و طلب خرقة. فلما أتوه

بها شدّها على جراحته، و لبس فوقها قلنسوة أخرى و اعتمّ عليها. و رجع عنه

شمر بن ذي الجوشن و من كان معه إلى مواضعهم، فمكث هنيهة ثم عاد و عادوا

إليه و أحاطوا به.

He threw his headpiece and wore a skullcap, wearing a turban over it. At this point, he had become weary and overburdened [by his wounds].

In some accounts: He threw down his headpiece, returned to the camp, and asked for a piece of cloth. When they brought one to him, he wrapped his wound with it, then wore a skullcap and wrapped a turban over it. Shimr ibn Thiljawshan and his men halted their advance and return to their positions. He rested for a while, then he returned to the battlefield and the enemy continued their advance, surrounding him.[101]

# Shimr Incites the Army to Fight

ثم نادى شمر: ما تنتظرون بالرجل فقد أثخنته السهام؟ فأحدقت به الرماح و

السيوف. فضربه رجل يقال له (زرعة بن شريك التميمي) ضربة منكرة، و رماه

(سنان بن أنس) بسهم في نحره، و طعنه (صالح بن وهب المّري) على خاصرته

طعنة منكرة، فسقط الحسين (عليه السلام) عن فرسه إلى الأرض، على خده

الأيمن. ثم استوى جالسا، و نزع السهم من نحره.

Shimr then called, "What are you waiting for? He's been overcome by
the arrows!" The swords and spears [of the enemy] surrounded him. A
man named Zur'a ibn Shurayk al-Tameemi struck him a deadly blow.
Sinan ibn Anas shot him with an arrow in his neck. Salih ibn Wahab
al-Murri gave him a fatal stab in his waist. Al-Hussain (a) fell off his
horse to the ground, falling on his right cheek. He sat up and drew the
arrow out of his neck.[102]

# Al-Hussain (a) Falls off his Horse

فجعل (عليه السلام) ينزع السهم بيده، و يتلقّى الدم بكفيه و يخضب به لحيته
و رأسه الشريف، و يقول:

[Al-Hussain (a)] drew the arrow out and began to take the flowing blood in his hands and using it to stain his noble head and beard. He would say,

هكذا ألقى ربي الله، و ألقى جدي رسول الله (صلى الله عليه و آله
و سلم)، و أشكو إليه ما نزل بي.

*This is how I will meet my Lord, God! This is how I will meet my grandfather, the Messenger of God (s), and complain to him of what befell me!*

و خرّ صريعا مغشيا عليه. فلما أفاق من غشيته وثب ليقوم للقتال فلم يقدر.
فبكى بكاء عاليا، و نادى:

He then fell unconscious. When he woke, he attempted to stand and fight, but could not. He cried out loudly and said,

وا جدّاه، وا محمداه، وا أبا القاسماه، وا أبتاه، وا علياه، وا حسناه، وا
جعفراه، وا حمزتاه، وا عقيلاه، وا عباساه، وا عطشاه، وا غوثاه، وا
قلة ناصراه. أقتل مظلوما و جدي محمّد المصطفى، و أذبح عطشانا و
أبي علي المرتضى، و أترك مهتوكا و أمي فاطمة الزهراء (عليها السلام)!

*O' grandfather! O' Muhammad (s)! O' Abu al-Qasim (s)! O' father!
O' Ali (a)! O' Hassan (a)! O' Ja'far! O' Hamza! O' Aqeel! O'
Abbas! O' [how strong is] my thirst! O' [who will come to my] aid! O'
how few are my supporters! Will I be oppressed and killed while my*

*grandfather is Muhammad al-Mustafa (s)? Will I be slaughtered thirsty while my father is Ali al-Murtada (a)? Will I be left massacred while my mother is Fatima al-Zahraa (a)?*[103]

# Al-Hussain (a) Fights on his Feet

كانت عليه جبّة من خز، و كان معتمّا، و كان مخضوبا بالوسمة. قال: سمعته يقول

قبل أن يقتل، و هو يقاتل على رجليه قتال الفارس الشجاع:

He [al-Hussain (a)] was wearing a woolen coat and a turban, and [was
marked by the blood of the wounds that covered his body]. I heard
him say before he was killed, as he was fighting on his feet like a valiant
warrior.'" [Al-Hussain (a) then said,]

أعلى قتلي تحاثّون؟! أما و الله لا تقتلون بعدي عبدا من عباد الله،
الله أسخط عليكم لقتله مني. و ايم الله إني لأرجو أن يكرمني الله
بهوانكم، ثم ينتقم لي منكم من حيث لا تشعرون. أما و الله إن قتلتموني
لقد ألقى الله بأسكم بينكم و سفك دماءكم، ثم لا يرضى لكم حتى
يضاعف لكم العذاب الأليم.

*You encourage each other to kill me?! By God, you will never kill
another of God's servant for which His anger will be greater than for
your killing me! By God, I hope that God will honor me by your demise
and then take reribution for [my murder] from whence you are not aware!
Indeed, by God, if you kill me, God will turn your enmity toward one
another, [so that you] shed [each other's] blood. He will not be content
until He multiplies the most painful punishment [that you have now
earned].* [104]

# The Martyrdom of Muhammad ibn Abu Saeed ibn Aqeel

قال هاني بن ثبيت الحضرمي: إني لواقف عاشر عشرة لما صرع الحسين (عليه السلام)، إذ نظرت إلى غلام من آل الحسين (عليه السلام)، عليه إزار و قميص، و في أذنيه درّتان، و بيده عمود من تلك الأبنية، و هو مذعور يتلفّت يمينا و شمالا. فأقبل رجل يركض، حتى إذا دنا منه مال عن فرسه، و علاه بالسيف و قطعه. فلما عيب عليه كفّى عن نفسه. و ذلك الغلام هو محمّد بن أبي سعيد بن عقيل بن أبي طالب (عليه السلام) و كانت أمه تنظر إليه و هي مدهوشة.

Hani ibn Thubait al-Hadrami said, "I was standing [among the Umayyad soldiers] on the tenth [of Muharram] when al-Hussain (a) was felled. Suddenly, I saw a boy from the family of al-Hussain (a) wearing [...] two pearls in his ears and carrying a pillar from one of the tents. He was terrified, turning left and right. A man rushed towards him. When he got near the boy, he leaned off his horse and struck him with his sword, killing him. When he was chided for his actions, he refused to give his name [so that he would not be known]."

That boy was Muhammad ibn Abu Saeed ibn Aqeel ibn Abu Talib. His mother was watching him in shock [as he was killed].[105]

# The Martyrdom of Abdullah al-Asghar ibn al-Hassan (a)

ثم إنهم لبثوا هنيئة و عادوا إلى الحسين (عليه السلام) و أحاطوا به، و هو جالس على الأرض لا يستطيع النهوض. فخرج الغلام عبد الله بن الحسن السبط (عليه السلام) و له إحدى عشرة سنة، و نظر إلى عمه و قد أحدق به القوم، فأقبل من عند النساء يشتدّ نحو عمه الحسين (عليه السلام)، فلحقته زينب (عليها السلام) لتحبسه، فقال لها الحسين (عليه السلام):

After a while, they returned to al-Hussain (a) and surrounded him as he was sitting on the ground unable to stand. A young boy, Abdullah ibn al-Hassan al-Sibt (a), ran out and he was eleven years of age. He saw his uncle surrounded by soldiers. He ran from amongst the women, rushing toward his uncle al-Hussain (a). [Lady] Zainab (a) ran after him to hold him. Al-Hussain (a) said to her,

احبسيه يا أختي.

*Hold him back, sister!*

فأبى و امتنع عليها امتناعا شديدا، و قال: و الله لا أفارق عمي. و أهوى أبجر ابن كعب إلى الحسين (عليه السلام) بالسيف، فقال له الغلام: ويلك يابن الخبيثة، أتقتل عمي؟ فضربه أبجر بالسيف، فاتّقاها الغلام بيده، فأطنّها إلى الجلد، فإذا هي معلّقة. فصاح الغلام: يا عمّاه. فأخذه الحسين (عليه السلام) فضمّه إليه، و قال:

The boy refused and tried as best he can to escape her.

[When the boy saw that] Abjar ibn Ka'b came close to al-Hussain (a) with his sword, he called out, "Woe to you, son of a vile woman! Would you kill my uncle?" Abjar struck [Abdullah] with his sword. When the boy tried to block the blow with his hand, it severed his arm so that it hung only by the skin. The boy cried out, "Uncle!" Al-Hussain (a) took him close and said,

يا بن أخي اصبر على ما نزل بك، و احتسب في ذلك الخير، فإن الله يلحقك بآبائك الصالحين.

*O' nephew, be patient with what has befallen you and await the best of rewards for it! Surely, God will allow you to join your righteous forefathers.*

و رفع الحسين (عليه السلام) يديه قائلا:

Al-Hussain (a) then raised his hand and said,

اللّهم إن متّعتهم إلى حين، ففرّقهم تفريقا، و اجعلهم طرائق قددا [أي مذاهب متفرقة]، و لا ترض الولاة عنهم أبدا، فإنهم دعونا لينصرونا، ثم عدوا علينا يقاتلوننا.

*O' God, if You will provide for them for a while, then seperate them into factions, make them into various sects, and do not let the governors be pleased with them. Surely, they called us to support us, but they turned against us and fought us!*

و رمى حرملة بن كاهل الغلام بسهم فذبحه و هو في حجر عمّه. و حملت الرجّالة يمينا و شمالا على من كان بقي مع الحسين (عليه السلام) فقتلوهم، حتى لم يبق معه إلا ثلاثة نفر أو أربعة.

Harmala ibn Kahil launched an arrow at the boy, killing him in his uncle's arms. The [enemy] infantry charged left and right and killed anyone who remained with al-Hussain (a). None remained at that point but three or four men [alongside al-Hussain (a)].[106]

## Lady Zaynab Speaks to Omar ibn Saad

و خرجت أخته زينب (عليها السلام) إلى باب الفسطاط، فنادت عمر بن سعد

بن أبي وقاص: ويلك يا عمر، أيقتل أبو عبد الله و أنت تنظر إليه! فلم يجبها

عمر بشيء. فنادت: و يحكم أما فيكم مسلم ؟! فلم يجبها أحد بشيء.

[Lady] Zaynab walked to the tent's entrance and called out to Omar ibn Saad, "Woe to you, Omar! Will Abu Abdullah (a) be killed while you look on?!" He did not answer her, so she called out to the army, "Woe to you! Is there no Muslim amongst you?!" Again, no one answered.[107]

# Al-Hussain (a) Sees his Grandfather in a Vision

فخفق الحسين (عليه السلام) برأسه خفقة، ثم انتبه و هو يقول:

Al-Hussain (a) then lowered his head for a bit [as if he had slept for a short while]. He then awoke and said,

رأيت الساعة جدي رسول الله (صلى الله عليه و آله و سلم) و هو
يقول: يا بني اصبر، الساعة تأتي إلينا.

*I just saw my grandfather, the Messneger of God (s), and he said, 'My son, have patience. Soon, you will be with us.'* [108]

# The Men Who Killed al-Hussain (a) When he was Weakened

و نادى شمر بن ذي الجوشن الفرسان و الرجالة، فقال: و يحكم ما تنتظرون بالرجل (اقتلوه) ثكلتكم أمهاتكم؟. فحملوا عليه من كل جانب. فضربه زرعة بن شريك على كتفه اليسرى، و ضرب الحسين (عليه السلام) زرعة فصرعه. و ضربه آخر على عاتقه المقدس بالسيف ضربة كبا بها لوجهه، و كان قد أعيى، و جعل ينوء و يكبّ.

Shimr ibn Thiljawshan called out to his cavalry and infantry, "Woe to you, what are you waiting for? [Kill] the man! May your mothers grieve for you!" They attacked al-Hussain (a) from every direction. Zar'a ibn Shuraik struck al-Hussain (a) on his left shoulder. Al-Hussain (a) struck back and killed Zar'a. Another man struck him on his noble shoulder [again], so he fell [off his horse] to the ground. He had been overpowered, burdened [by his wounds] and felled.

فطعنه سنان بن أنس بن عمرو النخعي في ترقوته. ثم انتزع الرمح، فطعنه في بواني صدره. ثم رماه سنان أيضا بسهم فوقع السهم في نحره، فسقط (عليه السلام) و جلس قاعدا. فنزع السهم من نحره، و قرن كفيه جميعا، فكلما امتلأتا من دمائه خضّب بها رأسه و لحيته، و هو يقول:

Sinan ibn Anas ibn Amr al-Nakha'i stabbed him in his shoulder blade. He took the spear and stabbed him again in his ribs. He took an arrow and shot him with an arrow, striking him in his neck. Al-Hussain (a) fell and sat on the ground. He drew the arrow from his neck and clasped his hands together [gathering the blood that flowed from his wounds]. Whenever his hands would fill with blood, he would take it to stain his head and beard, saying,

كذا ألقى الله مخضّبا بدمي، مغصوبا عليّ حقي.

*This is how I will meet God, stained with my own blood and usurped of my rights!*[109]

# The Massacre

# Shimr's Second Cry Inticing his Men to Kill al-Hussain (a)

و بقي الحسين (عليه السلام) مطروحا مليّا، و لو شاؤوا أن يقتلوه لفعلوا، إلا
أن كل قبيلة تتّكل على غيرها و تكره الإقدام... فصاح الشمر: ما وقوفكم و ما
تنتظرون بالرجل، و قد أثخنته السهام و الرماح، احملوا عليه. و ضربه زرعة بن
شريك على كتفه الأيسر، و رماه الحصين في حلقه و ضربه آخر على عاتقه، و
طعنه سنان بن أنس في ترقوته، ثم في بواني صدره، ثم رماه بسهم في نحره و
طعنه صالح بن وهب في جنبه.

Al-Hussain (a) remained lying on the ground for a while. If the enemy had wished to kill him, they could have. But each tribe would rely on the other and refuse to step forward. Al-Shimr called out, "Why do you [just] stand there? What are you waiting for? [Why don't you kill] the man, when he has been overburdened by wounds and arrows? Charge at him!"

Zar'a ibn Shuraik struck him on his left shoulder, al-Hossayn shot him with an arrow in his jaw, and another man struck him on his shoulder [again]. Sinan ibn Anas stabbed him in his shoulder blade and his ribs, then shot him with an arrow in his neck. Salih ibn Wahab stabbed him in his side.[110]

# Al-Hussain (a) Asks for Water in his Last Breaths

فاستسقى (عليه السلام) في تلك الحال ماء، فأبوا أن يسقوه. و قال له رجل:
لا تذوق الماء حتى ترد الحامية فتشرب من حميمها. فقال (عليه السلام):

In that condition, al-Hussain (a) asked for water. The enemies refused to give him. A man called out, "You will not taste water until you reach the scortching fire [of Hell] and drink its boiling waters!" Al-Hussain (a) replied,

أنا أرد الحامية فأشرب من حميمها! بل أرد على جدي رسول الله (ص)،
و أسكن معه في داره، في مقعد صدق عند مليك مقتدر، و أشرب
من ماء غير آسن ، و أشكو إليه ما ارتكبتم مني و فعلتم بي.

*Is it me who will reach the scortching fire [of Hell] and drink its boiling waters? No! I will reach my grandfather the Messenger of God (s) and live with him in his home [in Paradise], in the abode of truthfulness with an omnipotent King, and drink it's unstaling water! I will complain to him of how you transgressed against me and done to me!*

# Al-Hussain's (a) Prayer Before his Martyrdom

و لما اشتدّ به الحال (عليه السلام) رفع طرفه إلى السماء و قال:

When [al-Hussain's (a) condition became dire and he was taking his last breaths], he looked towads the heavens and said,

اللّهم متعال المكان، عظيم الجبروت، شديد المحال، غني عن الخلائق، عريض الكبرياء، قادر على ما يشاء. قريب الرحمة، صادق الوعد، سابغ النعمة، حسن البلاء. قريب إذا دعيت، محيط بما خلقت. قابل التوبة لمن تاب إليك. قادر على ما أردت، تدرك ما طلبت. شكور إذا شكرت، ذكور إذا ذكرت. أدعوك محتاجا، و أرغب إليك فقيرا، و أفزع إليك خائفا. و أبكي مكروبا، و أستعين بك ضعيفا، و أتوكل عليك كافيا.

*O' God, you are the Most High Place, Greatest Power, and Most Terrible Punishment. You are independent of all creation, sublime in Your glory, able to act as You wish, close [to Your creations] in Your mercy, truthful in Your promise, bounteous in Your blessings, and generous in Your goodness. Your are close if You are called upon and wil accept the repentance of whoever repents to You. You are able in what You will and will have what You demand. You are appreciative of those who thank You and will remember those who remember You. I call on You while I'm in need, long for You in my dependence [on You], seek refuge in You from my fears, cry [to You] in my distress, rely on You in my weakness, and trust in You to suffice me.*

اللّهم احكم بيننا و بين قومنا، فإنهم غرّونا و خذلونا و غدروا بنا و قتلونا، و نحن عترة نبيك و ولد حبيبك محمّد (صلى الله عليه و آله و

سلم) الّذي اصطفيته بالرسالة، و اتمنته على الوحي، فاجعل لنا من أمرنا فرجا و مخرجا، يا أرحم الراحمين. صبرا على قضائك يا رب، لا إله سواك، يا غياث المستغيثين. مالي ربّ سواك، و لا معبود غيرك. صبرا على حكمك. يا غياث من لا غياث له، يا دائما لا نفاد له. يا محيي الموتى، يا قائما على كل نفس بما كسبت، احكم بيني و بينهم و أنت خير الحاكمين.

*O' God, judge between us and our people, for they have called decieved, deserted, betrayed, and murdered us. We are the progeny of your Prophet and the children of your Beloved Muhammad (s), whom You had chosen for the message and trusted with revelation. So grant us in our matter relief and rescue, O' most merciful of the merciful. [Grant us] patience with Your judgment. There is no God but You, O' aid of those who call [upon You] for aid. I have no Lord but You and I do not worship anyone beside You, [so grant me] patience with Your judgment. O' aid of whomever has no aid [but You]! O' Everlasting who will never perish! O' reviver of the dead! O' judge of every soul and what it has done! Judge between me and them, for You are the best of the judges.*[111]

# Enemy Generals are Bewildered and Unable to Behead al-Hussain (a)

ثم غشي عليه، و بقي ثلاث ساعات من النهار، و القوم في حيرة لا يدرون أهو حيّ أم ميّت! قال: و بقي الحسين (عليه السلام) مكبوبا على الأرض ملطّخا بدمه ثلاث ساعات، و هو يقول:

[Al-Hussain (a)] then fell unconscious with the soldiers surrounding him for three hours, not knowing whether he was dead of alive. Al-Hussain (a) remained on laying on the ground for three hours, stained with his own blood. He would say,

**صبرا على قضائك، لا إله سواك، يا غياث المستغيثين.**

*[O' God, grant us] patience with Your judgment! There is no God but You, O' aid of whoever asks [You] for aid!*

فابتدر إليه أربعون رجلا كل منهم يريد حزّ نحره الشريف. و عمر بن سعد يقول: ويلكم عجّلوا عليه. و كان أول من ابتدر إليه (شبث بن ربعي) و بيده السيف، فدنا منه ليحتزّ رأسه، فرمق الحسين (عليه السلام) بطرفه، فرمى السيف من يده و ولّى هاربا، و هو يقول: ويحك يابن سعد، تريد أن تكون بريئا من قتل الحسين و إهراق دمه، و أكون أنا مطالب به! معاذ الله أن ألقى الله بدمك يا حسين.

Forty men approached him, attempting to sever his noble head. All the while, Omar ibn Saad would call out, "Woe to you! Finish him quickly!"

The first to approach [al-Hussain (a)] was Shabath ibn Rib'i carrying a sword. He came close to sever his head, but when al-Hussain (a) opened his eyes, [Shabath] threw down the sword and ran away saying,

"Woe to you, ibn Saad! You wish to claim innocence from the blood and murder of al-Hussain (a), while I would be the one responsible for it! God forbid that I should meet Him with your blood [on my hands], O' Hussain (a)!"

فأقبل (سنان بن أنس) و قال: ثكلتك أمك و عدموك قومك لو رجعت عن قتله. فقال شبث: يا ويلك إنه فتح عينيه في وجهي فأشبهتا عيني رسول الله (صلى الله عليه و آله و سلم) فاستحييت أن أقتل شبيها لرسول الله. فقال له: يا ويلك أعطني السيف فأنا أحقّ منك بقتله.

Sinan ibn Anas stepped forward and said [to Shabath], "May your mother mourn you and your tribe grieve for you if you refuse to kill him!" Sabath replied, "Woe to you! He opened his eyes when I drew near and they looked like the eyes of the Messenger of God (s). Shame did not allow me to kill a man who looked like the Messenger of God (s)." [Sinan] said, "Woe to you! Give me the sword, for I am more deserving [of the honor] to kill him then you!"

فأخذ السيف و همّ أن يعلو رأسه، فنظر إليه الحسين (عليه السلام) فارتعد سنان، و سقط السيف من يده و ولى هاربا، و هو يقول: معاذ الله أن ألقى الله أن ألقى الله بدمك يا حسين. فأقبل إليه (شمر) و قال: ثكلتك أمك ما أرجعك عن قتله؟. فقال: يا ويلك، إنه فتح في وجهي عينيه، فذكرت شجاعة أبيه، فذهلت عن قتله.

He took the sword, hoping to sever [al-Hussain's (a)] head. But when al-Hussain (a) looked at him, Sinan began to shake. The sword fell from his hand and he ran off, saying, "God forbid that I should meet him with your blood [on my hands], O' Hussain (a)!"

Shimr approached [Sinan] and said, "May your mother mourn you, why have you returned without killing him?" He replied, "Woe to you! He opened his eyes when I drew near, so I remembered the valor of his father and was too overcome to kill him!"[112]

# Who Will Finish Off al-Hussain (a)?

و قال سنان لخولي بن يزيد الأصبحي: احتزّ رأسه، فضعف و ارتعدت يداه. فقال له سنان: فتَّ الله عضدك و أبان يدك. فنزل إليه (شمر بن ذي الجوشن) و كان أبرص، فضربه برجله و ألقاه على قفاه ثم أخذ بلحيته. فقال له الحسين (عليه السلام):

Sinan [ibn Anas] said to Khawli ibn Yazid al-Asbahi, "Sever his head!" But he hesitated and his hands shook [in fear]. Sinan said to him, "May God ruin your arms and sever your hands!"

Then Shimr ibn Thiljawshan, who was a leper, came to al-Hussain (a), kicked him, threw him on his back, and grabbed his beard. Al-Hussain (a) said to him,

أنت الكلب الأبقع الّذي رأيته في منامي.

*You are the piebald dog I saw in my vision!*

قال شمر: أتنشبّهني بالكلاب يابن فاطمة؟. ثم جعل يضرب بسيفه مذبح الحسين (عليه السلام). و روي أنه جاء إليه شمر بن ذي الجوشن و سنان بن أنس، و الحسين (عليه السلام) بآخر رمق، يلوك بلسانه من العطش. فرفسه شمر برجله، و قال: يابن أبي تراب، ألست تزعم أن أباك على حوض النبي يسقي من أحبه؟. فاصبر حتى تأخذ الماء من يده.

Shimr says, "Do you liken me to a dog, O' son of Fatima (a)?" and began to strike al-Hussain's (a) neck with his sword.

It is also narrated that al-Hussain (a) was approached by Shimr ibn Thiljawshan and Sinan ibn Anas while he was taking his last breaths and chewing his tongue out of thirst. Shirm kicked him and said, "O' son of Abu Turab, do you not claim that your father stands at the Prophet's (s) Pond [in Paradise], giving water to whomever loves him? So wait until you take a drink from his hand."

ثم قال الشمر لسنان بن أنس: احتزّ رأسه من قفاه. فقال: و الله لا أفعل ذلك، فيكون جده محمّد خصمي. فغضب شمر منه، و جلس على صدر الحسين (عليه السلام) و قبض على لحيته، و همّ بقتله. فضحك الحسين (عليه السلام) و قال له:

Shimr then said to Sinan, "Sever his head from the back!" Sinan replied, "By God I will not do so, for his grandfather Muhammad (s) would be my adversary!" Shimr grew angry, sat on al-Hussain's (a) chest, held on to his bear, and proceeded to finish him. Al-Hussain (a) smiled and said,

أتقتلني! أو لا تعلم من أنا؟

*Will you kill me? Do you not know who I am?*

قال: أعرفك حق المعرفة؛ أمك فاطمة الزهراء، و أبوك علي المرتضى، و جدك محمّد المصطفى، و خصمك الله العليّ الأعلى، و أقتلك و لا أبالي. و ضربه الشمر بسيفه اثنتي عشرة ضربة، ثم حزّ رأسه الشريف.

Shimr replied, "I know you well. Your mother is Fatima al-Zahraa (a), your father is Ali al-Murtada (a), and your grandfather is Muhammad al-Mustafa (s), but your enemy is God the Most Hight and Sublime! I will kill you without hesitation!" Shimr struck al-Hussain (a) twelve times and then severed his noble head.[113]

# Shimr Beheads al-Hussain (a)

فقال الشمر لسنان: يا ويلك إنك لجبان في الحرب، هلمّ إليّ بالسيف فو الله ما أحد أحقّ مني بدم الحسين. إني لأقتله سواء أشبه المصطفى أو علي المرتضى. فأخذ السيف من يد سنان و ركب صدر الحسين (عليه السلام) فلم يرهب منه، و قال: لا تظنّ أني كمن أتاك، فلست أردّ عن قتلك يا حسين! فقال له الحسين (عليه السلام):

Shimr said to Sinan, "Woe to you! What a coward in the midst of battle. Give me the sword, for by God no one is more deservant of al-Hussain's (a) blood then I am. I will kill him whether he is the like of al-Mustafa (a) or Ali al-Murtada (a)!" He took the sword from Sinan's hand and sat on al-Hussain's (a) chest. But al-Hussain (a) did not show fear, so Shimr said, "Do not think that I am like the ones who came to you before, for I will not hesitate to kill you O' Hussain (a)!" Al-Hussain (a) said,

من أنت ويلك، فلقد ارتقيت مرتقى صعبا طالما طالما قبّله النبي (صلى الله عليه و آله و سلم).

*Woe to you, who are you? You have surely sat on a great place which the Prophet (s) would always kiss!*

فقال له: أنا الشمر الضبابي. فقال الحسين (عليه السلام):

Shimr [who had masked himself] replied, "I am al-Shimr al-Dababi." Al-Hussain (a) asked,

أما تعرفني ؟!

*Do you not know who I am?*

215

فقال ولد الزنا: بلى، أنت الحسين، و أبوك المرتضى، و أمك الزهرا، و جدك المصطفى، وجدتك خديجة الكبرى. فقال له:

The bastard replied, "Yes, you are al-Hussain (a), your father is al-Murtada (a), your mother is al-Zahraa (a), your grandfather is al-Mustafa (s), and your grandmother is Khadija al-Kubra." Al-Hussain (a) said,

ويحك إذا عرفتني فلم تقتلني ؟

*Woe to you, if you know me then why would you kill me?*

فقال له: أطلب بقتلك الجائزة من يزيد. فقال له الحسين (عليه السلام):

Shimr replied, "By killing you, I wish to earn the prize of Yazid." Al-Hussain (a) asked,

أيّا أحبّ إليك؛ شفاعة جدي رسول الله (صلى الله عليه و آله و سلم) أم جائزة يزيد؟

*Which is more preferable to you, the intercession of my grandfather the Messenger of God (s) or the prize of Yazid?*

فقال: دانق من جائزة يزيد أحب إليّ منك و من شفاعة جدك و أبيك. فقال له الحسين (عليه السلام):

Shimr replied, "A single coin from the prize of Yazid is more preferable to me than the intercession of your father and grandfather!" Al-Hussain (a) said,

إذا كان لا بدّ من قتلي فاسقني شربة من الماء.

*If you must kill me, then give me a drink of water first!*

فقال: هيهات هيهات، و الله ما تذوق الماء أو تذوق الموت غصّة بعد غصّة و جرعة بعد جرعة. ثم قال شمر: يابن أبي تراب، ألست ترعم أن أباك على الحوض يسقي من أحبّ، اصبر قليلا حتى يسقيك أبوك. فقال له (عليه السلام):

Shimr said, "Alas! Alas! You will not taste water until you taste death [slowly by my hand]! O' son of Abu Turab (a), do you not claim that your father is at the Pond [of Paradise], quenching the thirst of whomever he likes? So wait a little until your father gives you a drink!" Al-Hussain (a) said,

سألتك بالله إلا ما كشفت لي عن لثامك لأنظر إليك.

*I ask you by God to lift your mask so that I can see your face!*

فكشف له عن لثامه، فإذا هو أبرص أعور، له بوز كبوز الكلب، و شعر كشعر الخنزير. فقال له الإمام (عليه السلام):

When Shimr lifted his mask, al-Hussain (a) saw that he was a leper and was blind in one eye, having a long nose like the snout of a dog and hair like the hair of a pig. Al-Hussain (a) said,

صدق جدي رسول الله (صلى الله عليه و آله و سلم).

*Surely, my grandfather the Messenger of God (s) has told the truth!*

فقال له الشمر: و ما قال جدك رسول الله (صلى الله عليه و آله و سلم)؟ قال:

Shimr asked, "And what has your grandfather the Messenger of God (s) said?" Al-Hussain (a) replied,

سمعته يقول لأبي (عليه السلام): يا علي يقتل ولدك هذا أبرص أعور، له بوز كبوز الكلب، و شعر كشعر الخنزير.

*I heard him say to my father, 'O' Ali (a), this son of yours [i.e. al-Hussain (a)] will be killed by a leper who is blind in one eye, having a long nose like the snout of a dog and hair like the hair of a pig.*

فقال له شمر: يشبّهني جدك رسول الله بالكلاب، و الله لأذبحتك من القفا، جزاء لما شبّهني جدك. ثم أكبّه على وجهه، و جعل يحزّ أوداجه بالسيف [...]و كلما قطع منه عضوا نادى الحسين (عليه السلام):

Shimr said, "Does your grandfather the Messenger of God (s) liken me to a dog! By God, I will slaughter you from the back as punishment for the words of your grandfather!" Shimr then turned al-Hussain (a) on his face and began to slit his veins with the sword [...]. Whenever Shimr severed a part of him, al-Hussain (a) cried out,

وا محمداه وا علياه وا حسناه وا جعفراه وا حمزتاه وا عقيلاه وا عباساه وا قتيلاه وا قلة ناصراه وا غربتاه.

*O' Muhammad (s)! O' Ali (a)! O' Hassan (a)! O' Ja'far! O' Hamza! O' Aqeel! O' Abbas! O' the murder! O' how few my supporters are! O' how distant I am from home!*

فاحتزّ الشمر رأسه الشريف، و علاه على قناة طويلة .. فكبّر العسكر ثلاث تكبيرات.

Shimr severed al-Hussain's (a) head and hoisted it on a long spear. The army cried out thrice, "*Allah Akbar*!"[114]

# The Number of al-Hussain's (a) Wounds

ثم عدّوا ما في جسد الحسين (عليه السلام)، فوجدوه ثلاثا و ثلاثين طعنة برمح، و أربعا و ثلاثين ضربة بالسيف. و وجدوا في ثيابه مائة و عشرين رمية بسهم.

When they counted the number of wounds in al-Hussain's (a) body, they found 33 spear stabs and 34 sword cuts. They found on his clothes 120 arrow holes.

# Al-Hussain's (a) Horse at the Moment of his Martyrdom

و لما صرع الحسين (عليه السلام) جعل فرسه يحامي عنه، و يثب على الفارس [أي من الأعداء] فيخبطه عن سرجه و يدوسه، حتى قتل الفرس أربعين رجلاً، كما في (مدينة المعاجز) عن الجلودي. ثم تمرّغ الفرس في دم الحسين (عليه السلام) و أقبل يركض نحو خيمة النساء و هو يصهل. فسمعت بنات النبي (صلى الله عليه و آله و سلم) صهيله فخرجن، فإذا الفرس بلا راكب، فعرفن أن حسينا (عليه السلام) قد قتل.

When al-Hussain (a) was felled, his horse began to defend him. It would jump at every enemy rider, push him off his saddle, and trample him, until it killed forty men (as narrated by al-Jaloudi in *Madinat al-Ma'ajiz*).

The horse then stained its mane with al-Hussain's (a) blood and galloped toward the camp, neighing loudly. The daughter's of the Prophet (s) heard his neighs and stepped out [to greet al-Hussain (a)]. When they saw that the horse returned without a rider, they knew that al-Hussain (a) was killed.[115]

# A Caller from the Heavens Warns a Misguided Nation

قال أبو عبد الله الصادق (عليه السلام):

Imam Sadiq (a) said,

لما ضرب الحسين بن علي (عليها السلام) بالسيف، ثم ابتدر [شمر] ليقطع رأسه، نادى مناد (بعض الملائكة) من قبل الله رب العزّة تبارك و تعالى، من بطنان العرش، فقال: ألا أيتها الأمة المتحيّرة الظالمة الضالّة بعد نبيّها (القاتلة عترة نبيّها)، لا وقّكم الله (لصوم) و لا فطر و لا أضحى. لا جرم و الله ما وفّقوا و لا يوفّقون أبدا، حتى يقوم ثائر الحسين (عليه السلام).

*When al-Hussain ibn Ali (a) was struck with the sword and Shimr approached to sever his head, a caller [an angel] called by the command of God, the Blessed and Almighty Lord of Majesty, from the vicinity of the Throne, 'O' nation that has become confused, oppressive, and deviant after it's Prophet (s), may God never bless you with a fast, a Fitr, or an Adha.' By God, surely they were not blessed nor will they ever be blessed until the rising of the one will seek vengence for al-Hussain (a) [meaning the Awaited Twelfth Imam (a)].[116]*

# A Caller from the Heavens Mourns al-Hussain (a)

يقول أبو مخنف: إن (الشمر) لما شال الرأس الشريف في رمح طويل، و كبّر العسكر ثلاث تكبيرات؛ زلزلت الأرض، و أظلمت السموات، و قطرت السماء دما. و نادى مناد من السماء: قتل و الله الإمام ابن الإمام أخو الإمام. قتل و الله الهمام بن الهمام، الحسين بن علي بن أبي طالب (عليه السلام). فارتفعت في ذلك الوقت غبرة شديدة سوداء مظلمة، فيها ريح حمراء، لا يرى فيها عين و لا أثر، حتى ظنّ القوم أن العذاب قد جاء. فلبثوا كذلك ساعة ثم انجلت عنهم.

Abu Mikhnaf says that when al-Shimr hoisted the blessed head on a long spear and the enemy called out *Takbir* three times, the earth quaked, the heavens darkened, and the sky rained blood. A caller from the heavens called, "By God, an Imam - the son of an Imam and brother to an Imam - has been killed. By God, a valiant knight - son to a valiant knight - has been killed. He is al-Hussain ibn Ali ibn Abi Talib (a)." Then, a dark dust cloud rose carrying red sand. No thing or movement could be seen in it. People thought that [God's] punishment had befallen them. They were in that state for an hour until [the dust cloud] dissipated.[117]

# Notes

[1] Al-Muqarram, *Maqtal al-Hussain (a)*, 278.

[2] Al-Ha'eri, *al-Faji'a al-'Uthma*, 67.

[3] Al-Muqarram, *Maqtal al-Hussain (a)*, 232.

[4] Al-Ameen, *Lawa'ij al-Ashjan*, 116.

[5] Al-Khowarizmi, *Maqtal al-Hussain (a)*, 2:9.

[6] Al-Qazwini, *Al-Watha'eq al-Rasmiyya*, 162.

[7] Ibn Tawus, *Al-Luhuf*, 42.

[8] Al-Khowarizmi, *Maqtal al-Hussain (a)*, 2:14.

[9] Al-Muqarram, *Maqtal al-Hussain (a)*, 296.

[10] Al-Mufid, *Al-Irshad*, 236.

[11] Al-Muqarram, *Maqtal al-Hussain (a)*, 297.

[12] Al-Mufid, *Al-Irshad*, 237.

[13] Al-Muqarram, *Maqtal al-Hussain (a)*, 297.

[14] Al-Muqarram, *Maqtal al-Hussain (a)*, 299.

[15] Al-Muqarram, *Maqtal al-Hussain (a)*, 300.

[16] Al-Khowarizmi, *Maqtal al-Hussain (a)*, 2:11.

[17] Al-Khowarizmi, *Maqtal al-Hussain (a)*, 2:10.

[18] Al-Majlisi, *Muqaddimat Mir'aat al-'Uqool*, 2:253.

[19] Abu Mikhnaf, *Maqtal al-Hussain (a)*, 64.

[20] Al-Majlisi, *Muqaddimat Mir'aat al-'Uqool*, 2:254.

[21] Al-Majlisi, *Muqaddimat Mir'aat al-'Uqool*, 2:255.

[22] Al-Majlisi, *Muqaddimat Mir'aat al-'Uqool*, 2:255.

[23] Al-Ameen, *Lawa'ij al-Ashjan*, 142.

[24] Al-Tabari, *al-Tareekh*, 6:255.

[25] Al-Mufid, *Al-Irshad*, 238.

[26] Al-Khowarizmi, *Maqtal al-Hussain (a)*, 2:17; Abu Mikhnaf, *Maqtal al-Hussain (a)*, 65; Al-Muqarram, *Maqtal al-Hussain (a)*, 301.

[27] Al-Muqarram, *Maqtal al-Hussain (a)*, 301.

[28] Abu Mikhnaf, *Maqtal al-Hussain (a)*, 66.

[29] Al-Khowarizmi, *Maqtal al-Hussain (a)*, 2:17.

[30] Al-Khowarizmi, *Maqtal al-Hussain (a)*, 2:17.

[31] Abu Mikhnaf, *Maqtal al-Hussain (a)*, 67.

[32] Al-Muqarram, *Maqtal al-Hussain (a)*, 305.

[33] Al-Muqarram, *Maqtal al-Hussain (a)*, 305.

[34] Al-Khowarizmi, *Maqtal al-Hussain (a)*, 2:20.

[35] Al-Muqarram, *Maqtal al-Hussain (a)*, 306.

[36] Al-Muqarram, *Maqtal al-Hussain (a)*, 307.

[37] Al-Muqarram, *Maqtal al-Hussain (a)*, 312.

[38] Abu Mikhnaf, *Maqtal al-Hussain (a)*, 138.

[39] Al-Khowarizmi, *Maqtal al-Hussain (a)*, 2:24.

[40] Al-Muqarram, *Maqtal al-Hussain (a)*, 311.

[41] Al-Khowarizmi, *Maqtal al-Hussain (a)*, 2:23.

[42] Al-Khowarizmi, *Maqtal al-Hussain (a)*, 2:14.

[43] Al-Khowarizmi, *Maqtal al-Hussain (a)*, 2:14.

[44] Al-Khowarizmi, *Maqtal al-Hussain (a)*, 2:17.

[45] Al-Khowarizmi, *Maqtal al-Hussain (a)*, 2:17.

[46] Al-Khowarizmi, *Maqtal al-Hussain (a)*, 2:18.

[47] Al-Muqarram, *Maqtal al-Hussain (a)*, 313.

[48] Al-Khowarizmi, *Maqtal al-Hussain (a)*, 2:18.

[49] Al-Khowarizmi, *Maqtal al-Hussain (a)*, 2:19.

[50] Al-Khowarizmi, *Maqtal al-Hussain (a)*, 2:20.

[51] Al-Muqarram, *Maqtal al-Hussain (a)*, 294.

[52] Al-Ameen, *Lawa'ij al-Ashjan*, 146.

[53] Al-Khowarizmi, *Maqtal al-Hussain (a)*, 2:21.

[54] Al-Khowarizmi, *Maqtal al-Hussain (a)*, 2:21.

[55] Al-Muqarram, *Maqtal al-Hussain (a)*, 308.

[56] Al-Ameen, *Lawa'ij al-Ashjan*, 148.

[57] Al-Ameen, *Lawa'ij al-Ashjan*, 147.

[58] Al-Ameen, *Lawa'ij al-Ashjan*, 148.

[59] Al-Ameen, *Lawa'ij al-Ashjan*, 148.

[60] Al-Muqarram, *Maqtal al-Hussain (a)*, 315.

[61] Al-Khowarizmi, Maqtal al-Hussain (a), 2:25.

[62] Al-Khowarizmi, Maqtal al-Hussain (a), 2:26.

[63] Al-Muqarram, *Maqtal al-Hussain (a)*, 318.

[64] Al-Khowarizmi, Maqtal al-Hussain (a), 2:30.

[65] Al-Ha'eri, *Al-Faji'a al-'Uthma*, 137.

[66] Al-Ameen, *Lawa'ij al-Ashjan*, 152.

[67] Al-Ameen, *Lawa'ij al-Ashjan*, 152.

[68] Al-Ameen, *Lawa'ij al-Ashjan*, 174.

[69] Al-Ameen, *Lawa'ij al-Ashjan*, 152.

[70] Beydoun, *Mawsu'at Karbala*, 2:124.

[71] Beydoun, *Mawsu'at Karbala*, 2:124.

[72] Al-Ameen, *Lawa'ij al-Ashjan*, 175.

[73] Al-Muqarram, *Maqtal al-Hussain (a)*, 330.

[74] Al-Ameen, *Lawa'ij al-Ashjan*, 173-4.

[75] Al-Ameen, *Lawa'ij al-Ashjan*, 178.

[76] Al-Ameen, *Lawa'ij al-Ashjan*, 179.

[77] Al-Muqarram, *Maqtal al-Hussain (a)*, 334.

[78] Al-Ha'eri, *Al-Faji'a al-'Uthma*, 146.

[79] Al-Muqarram, *Maqtal al-Hussain (a)*, 335.

[80] Al-Zinjani, *Wasilat al-Darain*, 278.

[81] Al-Muqarram, *Maqtal al-Hussain (a)*, 340.

[82] Al-Turaihi, *Al-Muntakhab*, 450.

[83] Abu Mikhnaf, *Maqtal al-Hussain (a)*, 84.

[84] Al-Darabandi, *Asrar al-Shahada*, 423.

[85] Al-Muqarram, *Maqtal al-Hussain (a)*, 340.

[86] Al-Muqarram, *Maqtal al-Hussain (a)*, 341.

[87] Abu Mikhnaf, *Maqtal al-Hussain (a)*, 84.

[88] Abu Mikhnaf, *Maqtal al-Hussain (a)*, 86.

[89] Al-Qirmani, *Akhbar al-Duwal*, 107.

[90] Ibn Tawus, *Al-Luhuf*, 66.

[91] Al-Shabrawi, *Al-Ithaf*, 73.

[92] Al-Ha'eri, *Al-Faji'a al-'Uthma*, 105.

[93] Al-Khowarizmi, *Maqtal al-Hussain (a)*, 2:33.

[94] Al-Jawahiri, *Mutheer al-Ahzan*, 86.

[95] Al-Muqarram, *Maqtal al-Hussain (a)*, 348.

[96] Al-Khowarizmi, *Maqtal al-Hussain (a)*, 2:34.

[97] Abu Mikhnaf, *Maqtal al-Hussain (a)*, 89.

[98] Al-Majlisi, *Muqaddimat Mir'aat al-'Uqool*, 2:282.

[99] Al-Muqarram, *Maqtal al-Hussain (a)*, 346.

[100] Al-Khowarizmi, *Maqtal al-Hussain (a)*, 2:34.

[101] Al-Khowarizmi, *Maqtal al-Hussain (a)*, 2:35.

[102] Al-Khowarizmi, *Maqtal al-Hussain (a)*, 2:35.

[103] Al-Ha'eri, *Al-Faji'a al-'Uthma*, 167.

[104] Al-Majlisi, *Muqaddimat Mir'aat al-'Uqool*, 2:283.

[105] Al-Muqarram, *Maqtal al-Hussain (a)*, 353.

[106] Al-Muqarram, *Maqtal al-Hussain (a)*, 354.

[107] Al-Mufid, *Al-Irshad*, 242.

[108] Sibt ibn Al-Jawzi, *Tathkirat al-Khawas*, 263.

[109] Ibn Tawus, *Al-Luhuf*, 52.

[110] Al-Muqarram, *Maqtal al-Hussain (a)*, 354.

[111] Al-Muqarram, *Maqtal al-Hussain (a)*, 356.

[112] Abu Mikhnaf, *Maqtal al-Hussain (a)*, 89.

[113] Al-Khowarizmi, *Maqtal al-Hussain (a)*, 2:36.

[114] Abu Mikhnaf, *Maqtal al-Hussain (a)*, 91.

[115] Al-Mayaniji, *Al-'Uyoon al-'Abra*, 193.

[116] Al-Nisabouri, *Rawdat al-Wa'edhin*, 193.

[117] Al-Darabandi, *Asrar al-Shahada*, 429.

www.ingramcontent.com/pod-product-compliance
Lightning Source LLC
Chambersburg PA
CBHW021224090426
42740CB00006B/367

*9781943393329*